A
DICTIONARY
OF GOOD
ENGLISH

A Guide to Current Usage

S. G. McKASKILL

Edited by
Joan van Emden

First published 1977 by
Inkata Press Proprietary Limited
Melbourne

Published with revisions 1981 by
THE MACMILLAN PRESS LTD
Companies and representatives throughout the world

ISBN 0 333 30883 2

Printed in Hong Kong

INTRODUCTION TO REVISED EDITION

This book is intended to help everybody who wants to speak or write good, clear English. The dictionary arrangement makes reference easy – to find out what a simile is, look under 'simile' – while the cross-references help in the search for more information. If the student wishes to check up on the use of quotation marks, he or she will be directed also to '**Direct, Indirect Speech**' for more detail and further examples.

Some points of usage are repeated because of their importance and because a student may need to examine a problem more than once to understand it fully. Thus, the very important and frequently confused relationship between a subject and its verb is dealt with under '**Agreement**', '**Collective Nouns**' and '**Singular or Plural?**'

The *Dictionary* includes a number of exercises of varying difficulty, with reference in each case to the appropriate section. Students working on their own can therefore check their progress, with '**Common Errors**' (answers provided) as an extra guide. Teachers will no doubt find the exercises useful for classwork.

The book is designed for teaching at various levels. The many examples and the exercises will be helpful at 'O' level, while the more detailed explanations will be of interest to students studying 'A' levels or BEC Higher or National Certificates. It is hoped, too, that more advanced students in universities and colleges will find the *Dictionary* a handy reference book for 'brushing up' their English usage. A discussion of style and clarity of expression is included as well as basic grammar and punctuation.

In the advice given, there is wide use of grammatical terminology, too often ignored today; the terms are explained and will help students in further reading. Similarly, there is a tendency towards 'enlightened conservatism', in that not only is the traditional and formal usage given, but also reference to what is not yet – and what is only just – acceptable. A distinction is made between what is appropriate to the spoken and to the written word, to the formal and the informal occasion.

The English language is a flexible, vivid instrument for the expression of ideas, and great writers have effectively broken most of the rules at one time or another. For most of us, knowledge and understanding of the rules form the basis of good writing, and the *Dictionary* is intended to help us all to become good – if not great – writers.

CONTENTS

INTRODUCTION

It is the purpose of this book to provide the information and advice needed by people who wish to speak and write English of a good standard.

Two virtues are claimed for the book. Firstly, it is written simply, and can be used by people for whom standard references are unintelligible. Any student who has reached senior secondary level should be able to use the book effectively, thereby improving his use of English. Secondly, it includes numerous exercises which provide a necessary motive for using the reference section. This feature greatly increases the practical value of the book, as a reference and as a textbook.

The *Dictionary* meets a need felt by several groups—secondary students and their teachers, students in teacher-training colleges and other tertiary institutions, persons employed in secretarial work or concerned with correspondence, and members of the public who simply wish to improve their English.

A Dictionary of Good English is arranged in two parts—a guide to current usage arranged in dictionary order, followed by exercises related to the points of usage discussed in the dictionary section.

Used as a reference on usage, the *Dictionary* provides immediate assistance for those who want to know, for example, when to use 'if' in preference to 'whether', the different uses of 'beside' and 'besides', where to place a question mark and a quotation mark when both occur together, or whether 'Tom and me' is correct in a given sentence.

For those who wish to use the *Dictionary* as a textbook on functional grammar, a basic course in English grammar is provided in the following sections and in other articles mentioned in cross-references: **Parts of speech, Noun, Pronoun, Verb, Adjective, Adverb, Preposition, Conjunction, Interjection, Sentences, Phrase, Participles, Case, Tense,** and **Agreement.** In addition, useful hints on writing are provided in the section **Style.**

A student who wishes to gain maximum assistance from the book should first study the sections mentioned as giving a foundation

1

course in grammar, and complete the exercises related to these sections. The section numbers in the righthand column allow quick identification of the exercises related to a particular section in the 'Dictionary'. The 'Study Guide' also directs attention to sections relevant to a basic course in functional grammar. After studying these foundation-building sections, the student can work progressively through the remaining exercises, referring to the relevant sections of the 'Dictionary' as he proceeds.

Some important points of usage are included in several sections to provide emphasis through spaced repetition. Thus the very important relationship between a subject and its verb is dealt with in a section headed **Agreement,** and given further attention under the headings, **Collective nouns** and **Singular or plural?**

All material that does not bear directly on the subject of good and correct English usage has been excluded. However, in the explanation of grammatical points it is impossible to avoid using certain technical terms and referring to some of the basic principles of grammar. Indeed, a knowledge of these terms is necessary for anyone who wishes to progress beyond the 'try-to-remember' stage in learning to use correct English. Terms used and principles referred to are explained, and every article should be intelligible to the reader either by itself or when read in conjunction with other articles to which cross-references are given.

Most of the material in the *Dictionary* is concerned with the quality of correctness. However, the term 'good English' implies other qualities—for example, breadth of vocabulary and discernment in the choice of words. Therefore, a number of items have been included to emphasize the need for care and discrimination in using words. These items deal with homonyms, synonyms, words expressing shades of a common meaning, and other words which may be confused.

No attempt has been made to provide 'instant', ready-made answers to the problems presented in the 'Exercises'. It is sounder educationally to require an effort on the part of the reader. But each section of the 'Dictionary' has been written to lead the inquirer almost infallibly to the correct answers.

A general conservatism characterizes the advice and information given. But it is, one hopes, an enlightened conservatism. Conventions that are now ignored by some writers of good standing are not recommended without some mention of the current trend, and terms or constructions that have only recently risen to respectability are given the nod of approval. But change in language must be controlled

2

to ensure stability. A trend to anarchy in the use of language will help nobody—least of all the student striving for proficiency in the art of communication.

STUDY GUIDE

Subject	Sections
NOUN	220, 231, 11, 14, 15, 18, 70, 110, 186, 199, 211, 222, 238, 240, 282, 290, 308.
PRONOUN	249, 30, 33, 41, 59, 115, 116, 121, 131, 157, 160, 183, 188, 209, 210, 214, 215, 225, 241, 267, 301, 326, 329, 330, 331, 340.
VERB	318, 231, 9, 14, 15, 16, 18, 31, 35, 41, 55, 57, 102, 104, 113, 125, 148, 150, 154, 156, 168, 173, 189, 190, 191, 197, 200, 206, 221, 230, 234, 244, 259, 263, 279, 280, 282, 287, 291, 300, 322, 324.
ADJECTIVE	10, 231, 1, 3, 13, 25, 42, 49, 76, 88, 89, 92, 102, 114, 120, 123, 130, 135, 138, 140, 151, 161, 167, 170, 172, 176, 179, 185, 198, 213, 224, 241, 242, 266, 303, 316, 330.
ADVERB	12, 231, 13, 23, 24, 36, 111, 155, 192, 212, 226, 252.
PREPOSITION	246, 231, 17, 27, 48, 50, 75, 79, 91, 105, 132, 137, 144, 145, 169, 195, 295.
CONJUNCTION	85, 28, 45, 46, 48, 56, 90, 122, 166, 216, 218, 273.
SENTENCES	276, 277, 26, 64, 68, 93, 128, 129, 153, 184, 205, 237, 250, 264, 292, 293, 299, 307, 314.
PUNCTUATION	251, 34, 58, 72, 74, 94, 103, 133, 147, 163, 177, 181, 182, 240, 255, 258, 275.
SPELLING	286, 14, 15, 20, 21, 22, 48, 51, 61, 77, 82, 88, 98, 92, 100, 101, 123, 127, 158, 162, 182, 197, 236, 238, 244, 247, 259, 263, 270, 271, 274, 289, 304, 309, 332, 341.
STYLE	2, 6, 26, 42, 47, 64, 66, 68, 71, 73, 128, 129, 143, 153, 175, 184, 205, 211, 213, 264, 276, 278, 281, 283, 292, 293, 298, 299, 314, 342.

The section 'Common Errors' (page 167) provides a ready means of testing a student's ability to use correct English, thereby indicating the use he should make of this Study Guide.

DICTIONARY

A

1 A, An (the indefinite article)

(i) The general rule is that 'an' is used instead of 'a' before a vowel or a silent 'h', *for example*, **an** *orange*, **an** *hour*, **an** *honour*.

(ii) If the vowel has the sound of 'w' or 'y', use 'a', *for example*, **a** *European tour*, **a** *one-sided match*, **a** *united effort*.

(iii) 'An' may be used before a sounded 'h' in an unaccented syllable, *for example*, **an** *heretical doctrine*, **an** *historic event*, **an** *habitual criminal*. This rule is not universally followed today, for example, 'a hotel' is often preferred to 'an hotel' which is considered old-fashioned.

(iv) Sometimes the choice of 'a' or 'an' depends on whether we pronounce the names of the letters, or the words in full, *for example*, *an R.A.F. plane*, *a Royal Air Force plane*.

(v) The article 'a' is used with the positive degree of the adjective in expressions such as 'as big **a** slice', 'as wise **a** man'. But it should not be used with the comparative; thus it should be omitted from 'no bigger a slice' and 'no wiser a man', *for example*, *He has as big a slice as I have*, *There is no wiser man alive today*.

2 Abbreviations

A. The following abbreviations are in common use:

A.D. = in the year of our Lord (Latin: *anno Domini*)

ad lib. = at pleasure (Lat. *ad libitum*)

a.m. = before noon (Lat. *ante meridiem*)

anon. = anonymous, author not known

ca. or c. = about or approximately when referring to dates (Lat. *circa*)

cf. = compare (Lat. *confer*)

c/o = care of

c.o.d. = cash on delivery

ed. = editor, edited, edition

e.g. = for example (Lat. *exempli gratia*)

et al. = and others, other things or writers (Lat. *et alia* for things; *et alii* for persons)

etc. = and the rest (Lat. *et cetera*)

5

et seq. = and that which follows (Lat. *et sequentia*)
ff. = and the following pages or verses
ibid. = the same, that is, the same reference or page (Lat. *ibidem*)
idem = the same, that is, same work and page as in previous footnote
i.e. = that is (Lat. *id est*)
infra = below when referring to text following
inst. = of the present month (Lat. *instant*)
loc. cit. = in the place already mentioned (Lat. *loco citato*)
MS. = manuscript
N.B. = note well, take notice (Lat. *nota bene*)
op. cit. = the work or book already mentioned (Lat. *opere citato*)
p., pp. = page, pages, for example, p. 29, pp. 84–93
p.a. = by the year (Lat. *per annum*)
passim = here and there, scattered among different pages
p.m. = after noon (Lat. *post meridiem*)
pro tem. = for the time being (Lat. *pro tempore*)
prox. = next month (Lat. *proximo*)
P.S. = postscript (Lat. *post scriptum* = written after)
q.v. = which see, directing the reader to a reference (Lat. *quod vide*)
R.S.V.P. = Please reply (French: *Repondez s'il vous plait.*)
[sic] = thus, placed after a quoted word or phrase containing an error which was in the original
stet = used to restore an item which has been struck out or deleted (Lat. *stet* = let it stand)
supra = above when referring to text
ult. = last month (Lat. *ultimo*)
viz. = namely (Lat. *videlicet*)

B. (i) Most abbreviations and contractions in writing are made in three ways:

   (a) **by curtailing a word**, that is by giving the beginning of the word then writing a full stop, *for example,* **Feb.** (*February*), **log.** (*logarithm*), **anon.** (*anonymous*), **Co.** (*Company*), **Capt.** (*Captain*), **etc.** (*et cetera*), **Ed.** (*Editor*), **adv.** (*adverb*), **Eliz.** (*Elizabeth*).

   (b) **by dropping part of the middle of a word**, while retaining the beginning and the last letter of the word. It is recommended that in abbreviations of this type the stop be omitted to let the reader know that the first and last letters given are those of the complete word, *for example,* **Ltd** (*Limited*), **do** (*ditto*), **Messrs**

(*Messieurs*), **maths** (*mathematics*), **logs** (*logarithms*), **bldg** (*building*), **Fr** (*Father*), **dept** (*department*), **hr** (*hour*), **Sgt** (*Sergeant*).

Some writers favour the use of a stop after abbreviations of this type on the ground of consistency, but weight of opinion now favours omission of the stop.

(c) **by writing the initial letter, followed by other letters which may suggest the general sound.** In these cases the full stop is used, indicating that the end of the word is missing, *for example*, **cm.** (*centimetre*), **kg.** (*kilogram*), **ml.** (*millilitre*).

(ii) Another group of shortened words presents a difficulty. It includes words which originated as abbreviations but have come to be accepted as words, and names, in their own right, *for example*, *zoo, pram, phone, pub, taxi, bus, Fred, Tom, Betty*. No stop is required after such words.

But in some cases people will argue whether this independent status has been reached, *for example, exam, prefab, fridge, script, bra, vet, polio*. When doubt persists this suggests that the abbreviated form is not widely accepted as a word in its own right and that a stop should be used. However many writers faced with such a debatable point of usage will simply omit the stop.

(iii) No stop is used

   (a) after ordinal numbers, *for example, 1st, 2nd, 3rd*, etc.

   (b) in the possessive form of an abbreviation, *for example, Smith and Co's products.*

(iv) In punctuating initials, a full stop is placed after each letter that stands for a full word, *for example, J. B. Smith*; *R.S.V.P.*; *O.H.M.S.*; *TV.* (*television*); *MS.* (*manuscript*).

The practice is increasing of omitting stops in the case of organizations which are generally known by the initials, and in cases where the initials are pronounced as a word, *for example, GPO*; *BBC*; *UNESCO*; *UNO*; *radar*.

(v) In certain contractions the apostrophe is used in place of omitted letters, *for example, isn't, can't, wouldn't, it's* (*it is*).

(vi) In formal writing, including the addressing of envelopes, the full forms should be used, *for example, Collins* **Street** (*not St.*); *Brighton* **Road** (*not Rd*). In the case of titles, usage is inconsistent; most writers refer to **Professor** Jones, but **Dr** Jones.

7

(vii) Writers of taste do not use certain abbreviations, *for example, Scarboro', altho', nightie, hankie, an invite (invitation), an ad., flu, Jap.*

3 Abnormal, Subnormal

The Latin prefix 'ab' means 'from' or 'off', so 'abnormal' means simply 'not normal'.

*Examples: Those strange growths on the plum tree are **abnormal**.*
*It is **abnormal** for a child to be born with six fingers on one hand.*

The prefix 'sub' means 'under'. 'Subnormal' means 'below normal standard, less than normal'.

*Example: The Smiths have a son who is mentally **subnormal**.*

4 Above

In place of 'the above comment', it is better to write, 'the comment already made'. Or the comment may be repeated in summary form, beginning, 'My remarks concerning . . . ', or 'The foregoing remarks concerning . . . '

5 Absolutely

This word is often used for emphasis or to express finality. It is used unnecessarily in '**absolutely** perfect', '**absolutely** disastrous', and so on. Words such as 'perfect' and 'disastrous' convey meaning effectively, and the use of 'absolutely' adds nothing to their meanings.

6 Abstract language

The use of an abstract vocabulary is necessary when we are discussing certain subjects such as philosophy and aesthetics. But in most situations concrete language should be preferred. Good writers use a judicious mixture of the abstract and the concrete. It is the over-use, rather than the use, of abstract language that deserves criticism. Badly used, it says at great length what could have been said more effectively in fewer words.

Examples: Abstract: *The construction of a complex of buildings and arenas for the staging of sporting events is under active consideration.*
Concrete: *The building of a sports centre is being considered.*
Abstract: *Every endeavour will be exerted to satisfy your requirements at the earliest date practicable.*
Concrete: *We shall fulfil your order as soon as possible*

7 Acquaint

'Let me **tell** you the facts' is less pretentious than 'Let me **acquaint** you with the facts'.

8 Actual

In these sentences 'actual' and 'actually' serve no purpose and should be omitted.
*Examples: The **actual** truth is that . . .*
*The trouble **actually** is that he quarrels with everybody.*

9 Add up to

*Correct: These figures **add up to** one hundred.*
*Incorrect: What this **adds up to** is that we are in serious danger.*
'What this means is . . . ' is better in the second example.

10 Adjective

A. An adjective is often called a describing word. When used with a noun, an adjective describes, or qualifies, or adds information about, the thing named by the noun. Note the different 'picture' that results from a change of adjectives in these two sentences.
*Example: **Angry** natives called to the **terrified** sailors.*
***Excited** natives called to the **laughing** sailors.*
Adjectives are of three main types, but they all have the same function—qualifying a noun by telling what kind, how many, or which one. The three groups of adjectives are:
(i) **descriptive** adjectives—*a **blue** dress, a **Dutch** ship, a **sad** story, a **broken** bottle, the **crying** child, the water is **cold**, the sky is **cloudy***
(ii) **limiting** adjectives—***three** eggs, the **last** chapter, his **second** attempt, **this** book, **those** books, **few** men, **little** hope, **my** hat, **their** car*
(iii) **interrogative** adjectives, used in asking questions—***What** bird is that? **Which** dress will you wear?*
B. **Common errors in the use of adjectives:**
(i) *The cars travelled very **slow** through the mud.* An adverb, 'slowly', is required instead of the adjective.
(ii) *John is the **tallest** of the two brothers.* To compare two things, use the comparative degree. *John is the **taller** of the two brothers.*
(iii) *A tiger is **more fiercer** than a jackal.* 'Fiercer' means more fierce; omit 'more' to avoid a double comparison.
(iv) *The shark is more dangerous than any creature in the sea.* This comparison makes sense if it is changed to 'any **other** creature'; otherwise it really says that sharks are more dangerous than sharks.

9

(v) *I had a **terrific** holiday last Easter.* Find a more descriptive adjective to describe the holiday.

(vi) *Put **them** books on the table.* 'Them' is a pronoun; the adjective 'those' is required here.

(vii) *He gave me the biggest half of the pie.* A pie has two halves of equal size. Say 'the **bigger** portion' (of two), or 'the **biggest** portion' (if there are more than two).

(viii) *He read the three first verses of the poem.* There is only one first verse; say '**first three** verses'.

(ix) *The **then** Prime Minister promised to reduce taxation.* 'Then' is an adverb; it should not be used as an adjective before a noun. 'The Prime Minister **at that time** . . . ', or 'The Prime Minister **of the day** . . . ', are acceptable alternatives.

(See also **Adverb and adjective** and **Comparison of adjectives**.)

11 Admission, Admittance

'Admit' has two meanings—'confess' and 'allow to enter'. When 'admit' means 'confess', the corresponding noun is 'admission'.

*Example: His **admission** of guilt did not surprise me.*

When 'admit' means 'allow to enter', the corresponding noun is again 'admission' in most cases. However, in a more formal or official context, 'admittance' is often used.

*Examples: The **admission** charge is 50p.*

*No **admittance** without a permit.*

12 Adverb

A. Adverbs modify or limit the meaning of verbs and other parts of speech. Most adverbs are formed from adjectives by adding '-ly'.

Examples:

Adjectives: *happy, neat, quiet*

Adverbs: *happily, neatly, quietly*

Exceptions are adverbs 'well' and 'fast' corresponding to adjectives 'good' and 'fast'.

When we say that an adverb modifies a verb, what is meant by 'modifying'? This really means 'clarifying'; an adverb clarifies the sense to be attached to the modified word. For example, the sentence, 'The girl danced' brings to the mind a rather vague picture. But when we add the adverb—'The girl danced clumsily' (or 'gracefully'), the picture comes to life because we have clarified the nature of the action.

(i) Adverbs denote time, *go **now***; place, *come **here***; manner, *write **neatly***; degree, *He was **almost** exhausted*; order, ***Firstly** I wish to say* . . .

10

(ii) Adverbs modify
   (a) verbs: *He worked* **carefully.**
   (b) adjectives: *That is a* **very** *difficult problem.*
       My soup is **too** *hot.*
   (c) other adverbs: *He plays* **extremely** *well.*
       The car was travelling **quite** *slowly.*
   (d) prepositions: *The bus is* **almost** *at the terminus.*

(iii) There are also interrogative adverbs, used to ask questions:
   When *did he arrive?*
   How *did you come?*

(iv) The common words 'yes' and 'no' are adverbs—of affirmation and negation respectively.

B. **Common errors in the use of adverbs:**

(i) *We travelled much* **more faster** *than the other cars.* As 'more faster' is a double comparison, omit 'more'.

(ii) *The little boy spoke very* **polite.** Adverbs should not be confused with adjectives. An adverb, 'politely', not the adjective 'polite', is required to tell how the boy spoke.

(iii) *The hunters* **never saw no** *lions.* There are two errors here. Avoid the double negative 'never ... no' which gives an unintended affirmative meaning. Say 'didn't see any' instead of 'never saw no'. *The hunters* **didn't see any** *lions.*

(iv) *I was* **that** *tired I* **couldn't hardly** *keep awake.* Again there are two errors. The word 'that' is an adjective, but here we need an adverb of degree, 'so'. Avoid the double negative 'couldn't hardly'. *I was* **so** *tired* **that I could hardly** *keep awake.*

(v) *Mr Brown* **only** *died last Sunday.* The adverb 'only' must be placed with care. The meaning intended is that Mr Brown died only last Sunday. (See also **Only.**)

13 Adverb and adjective

(i) Generally, an adjective qualifies a noun, as in *a* **neat** *writer, a* **strong** *swimmer, a* **graceful** *dancer*; and an adverb modifies a verb, as in *writes* **neatly**, *swims* **strongly**, *dances* **gracefully.**

(ii) But sometimes the adjective form is used instead of the adverb. In some sentences, the forms 'new-mown hay' or 'new-laid eggs' have come to be accepted as alternatives to 'newly-mown hay' or 'newly-laid eggs'.

Examples: I like the smell of **new-mown** *hay.*
   I asked for a dozen **new-laid** *eggs.*
   He is as innocent as a **new-born** *babe.*
   The people are enjoying their **new-won** *freedom.*

11

> *A **newly-painted** house may be much older than a **new painted** house.*

(iii) The adjective is sometimes used with an adverbial function where formerly the adverb only was considered correct.

*Examples: Don't speak so **loud**.*
*Still waters run **deep**.*

14 Advice, Advise

Certain words ending in '-ce' and '-se' are the cause of many spelling errors.

The words 'advice', 'practice', and 'licence' are nouns.

*Examples: I shall ask my lawyer for **advice**.*
* **Practice** is needed to improve your golf.*
* My **licence** is in my wallet.*

The corresponding verbs are 'advise', 'practise', and 'license'.

*Examples: I **advise** you to be careful.*
* You must **practise** to improve your golf.*
* The authorities refused to **license** him to drive a heavy vehicle.*

A hint to help you remember: 'Ice' is a noun; the words 'adv**ice**', 'pract**ice**', and 'licen**ce**', ending in 'ce', are also nouns.

15 Affect, Effect

'Affect' is a verb, and 'effect' is the corresponding noun.

*Examples: Does this dust **affect** your eyes?*
* What **effect** does this dust have on your eyes?*

'Effect' is also used as a verb, meaning 'to bring about'.

*Example: The new Principal hopes to **effect** a number of changes.*

16 Aggravate

'Aggravate' means 'make worse'; it does not mean 'annoy'.

*Examples: The loss of markets will **aggravate** our economic problems.*
* Cosmetics are likely to **aggravate** a skin complaint.*

Nevertheless, 'aggravate' in the sense of 'exasperate' is used in colloquial English, and may become accepted in that sense.

17 Agree

We agree **with** a person, and **to** a plan or proposal.

*Examples: I **agree with** you that the culprit should be punished.*
* I am sorry that I cannot **agree to** your proposal.*

18 Agreement

There are certain rules concerning the agreement of one word with another in the sentence. The most important rules concern the agreement of a verb with its subject.

A. (i) A singular subject takes a singular verb; a plural subject takes a plural verb.

*Examples: That **boy is** my brother.*
*Those **boys are** my brothers.*

(ii) A subject consisting of two singular nouns joined by 'and' becomes a plural subject and takes a plural verb.

*Example: Your **mother and father have** just arrived.*

Sometimes two subject nouns that are closely associated in the mind may be regarded as one unit requiring a singular verb.

*Examples: **Bread and butter is** often preferred to cakes.*
***Fish and chips is** a popular meal for children.*

(iii) Care is needed to determine whether two nouns in the subject refer to one thing or more than one. In sentence (*a*) the two nouns in the subject refer to one person, and a singular verb is required; in (*b*) the nouns refer to two persons, and the verb must be plural.

(*a*) *The captain and coach **has** been injured.*

(*b*) *The captain and the coach **have** both been injured.*

(iv) Sometimes a plural noun names a single thing; a singular verb is then required.

*Examples: Sons and Lovers **is** Lawrence's best-known novel.*
*The United States **is** the leading industrial nation.*

B. (i) If two singular nouns are given as alternative subjects, the verb is singular; if the alternatives are plural, the verb is also plural.

*Examples: Either Ann or Jane **has** left **her** purse here.*
*Neither Frank nor John **has** brought **his** bat.*
*Neither the lions nor the tigers **have** eaten the stale meat.*

(ii) When alternative subjects each require a different verb form, both verbs should be given, unless the result is unpleasantly awkward.

*Examples: Either **you are** or **I am** to drive the lorry.*
*Neither the coach nor the **players were** confident of success.*

Often it is better to avoid this difficulty by reframing the sentence.

Examples: Either you or I will drive the truck.
You are to drive the truck. If you can't, I shall.

(iii) When a singular subject is separated from its verb by a plural noun which enlarges the subject, a singular verb is required.

*Examples: A **pile** of boxes **was** blocking the passage.*
*His **chain** of shops **is** bringing him a very large income.*

(See also **Collective nouns** and **Singular or plural?**)

19 All

All is followed by 'of' when a pronoun follows, *for example, **all of** us, **all of** it, **all of** them*.
When the reference is to number, 'all' and 'all of' are both allowable, *for example, **all** his friends, **all of** his friends*.
When the reference is to amount, 'of' should not be used, *for example, **all** the pudding, **all** the time, **all** the way*.

20 All ready, Already

'All ready' (two words) means 'prepared'; 'already' (one word spelt with one 'l') is an adverb meaning 'before this time'.
*Examples: Are you **all ready** to set off?*
*Some of our friends have **already** gone.*

21 All right

'All right' is always written as two words. An expression such as, 'he seems all right again after his illness', is colloquial; it would not be used in serious writing.
Most standard works refer to 'alright' as a mis-spelling and therefore unacceptable. But a language which includes 'already', 'almost', 'altogether', 'always', and 'although' will surely accept 'alright' eventually.

22 All together, Altogether

'All together' (two words) means 'all in one place or at one time'. 'Altogether' (one word spelt with one 'l') is an adverb meaning 'completely'.
*Examples: You must start the song **all together.***
*Take these documents and file them **all together.***
*He has ignored us **altogether.***

23 Almost, Nearly

(i) In the past, guides to correct usage recommended the use of 'nearly' to give emphasis, as in "Good heavens! It's **nearly** midnight!" or "I had to bid **nearly** fifty pounds to buy this chair." Nowadays few people make this distinction; 'nearly' and 'almost' are both acceptable in these sentences.
(ii) Use 'nearly' to say that you came near to doing something, but for some reason you did not.
*Examples: I **nearly** ran into that foolish pedestrian.*
*I **nearly** offered to lend him the money.*
(iii) To show one's feeling or state of mind, use 'almost'.
*Examples: I **almost** wish I hadn't bothered to help him.*
*You could **almost** feel the hostility in the room.*

14

24 Also

'Also' is an adverb, and should be placed as near as possible to the word it is intended to modify.

Examples: (*a*) **You also** *are involved in this crime.*

           (*b*) *You are **also involved** in this crime.*

           (*c*) *You are involved in **this crime also.***

In (*a*), 'also' refers to 'you'—that is, you in addition to other persons. In (*b*), 'also' refers to 'involved'—involved in crime in addition to other troubles.

In (*c*), 'also' refers to 'crime'—this crime in addition to other crimes. As a general rule, avoid using 'also' to begin a sentence, clause or phrase. 'Also' should not be used to join clauses or phrases; 'and' is also required.

*Examples: He ate two sandwiches **and (also)** several cakes.*

         *He went for a walk **and also** did some shopping.*

25 Alternate, Alternative

'Alternate' means 'first one then the other'; 'alternative' suggests a choice.

*Examples: He goes to the football and to the races on **alternate** Saturdays.*

         *I have no **alternative** but to work on Saturdays.*

         *There are several **alternative** courses of action open to you.*

26 Ambiguity

An ambiguous sentence is of doubtful meaning because it can be interpreted in more than one way.

Examples: (*a*) *Your dog seems to like me better than you.*

           (*b*) *John told Charles that he had been elected captain.*

           (*c*) *When the nightwatchman disturbed the burglar he fired several shots at him.*

           (*d*) *There are some people who will worry about nothing at all.*

As these examples show, ambiguity is often the result of careless use of pronouns:

Example (*a*) Does this say that your dog likes me better than he likes you, or better than you like me?

Example (*b*) Who is the 'he' that was elected captain—John or Charles?

Example (*c*) Who fired the shots?

15

Example (d) Does this say that it takes very little to worry some people, or that some people don't worry even when there is serious trouble?

Ambiguity is easily avoided with a little care, for example, 'Your dog seems to like me better than he likes you', or '. . . better than you like me'.

27 Among, Between

The rule is '**between** two, **among** more than two', but modern usage permits 'between' when referring to two or more.

*Example: The three scouts collected nearly a hundred dollars **between** them.*

Both these words must be followed by a plural noun.

Correct: I lost my watch **among the weeds**. ('. . . in a heap of weeds' is also correct).

*There was a short interval **between acts**.*

Incorrect: I lost my watch **among a heap** of weeds.

There was a short interval **between each act**.

The American usage 'amongst' is also acceptable in English.

28 And

(i) 'And' is a co-ordinating conjunction. Units of a sentence that are joined by 'and' must be units of the same kind—both must be single words, phrases, or clauses. This sentence is incorrect. *He introduced me to a friend from London and whom he had often mentioned*. It is wrong because 'and' joins an adjective phrase and an adjective clause.

(ii) Students are sometimes told that they should never use 'and' to begin a sentence.

*Example: (a) The children splashed happily in the water. **And** the mother watched them.*

This is wrong. A second sentence should state a new idea; it should not merely continue the idea expressed in the first sentence. *(a)* should be written as one sentence.

*(b) The children splashed happily in the water **and** the mother watched them.*

Very occasionally, a sentence may begin with 'and' to give emphasis. This device can be effective, but only if its use is deliberate and rare.

29 And which

It is safe to use 'and which' only if a clause beginning with 'which', and referring to the same thing, has been used earlier in the sentence.

Correct: *This is a car which I like **and which** I will consider buying.*
Incorrect: *This is a house conveniently situated **and which** I might buy.*

30 Another, Each other

It is customary to use 'one another' when speaking of more than two, and 'each other' of two only. Nowadays this distinction is not strictly observed.
*Examples: The **children** were all chasing **one another**.*
*The **two boys** were chasing **each other**.*

31 Anticipate, Expect

These two words are not interchangeable. The meaning of 'anticipate' is 'forestall' or 'foresee and take appropriate action'.
*Examples: Our attack failed because the enemy **anticipated** it.*
*The full back **anticipated** the forwards' move and was able to prevent a score.*
Use 'expect' before a noun clause beginning 'that . . . '
*Example: I **expect that** she will return soon.*

32 Any

(i) It is incorrect to say, 'The Volga is longer than any river in Europe', because '**any** river in Europe' includes the Volga. Inclusion of the word 'other' before 'river' will correct the sentence.
(ii) *Drake and Nelson are probably the most famous of any of the British naval leaders.* This is clumsy; the words 'of any' or 'of any of the' should be deleted.

33 Anyone, Any one, Anybody

(i) The pronouns 'anyone' and 'anybody' are singular, and a pronoun or possessive referring to them should be singular.
*Examples: Has **anyone** a knife **he** can lend me?* ('he', not 'they')
*   **Anyone** who acts so selfishly **is** sure to lose **his** friends.* ('is . . . his', not 'are . . . their')
*   Would **anybody** in **his** right senses do such a thing?* ('his', not 'their')
(ii) When 'anyone' is used to refer to people in general and not in an individual sense, it means 'all people' and may take a plural verb.
*Example: **Anyone** can go to the beach carnival, **can't they?***
(iii) 'Anyone' (one word) is a pronoun; it is never followed by 'of'. We can say '**Anyone** can make a mistake', or, using two words, '**Any one** of us could have made the same mistake' and '**Any one** of those carpets would suit my room'.

17

34 Apostrophe

The apostrophe has three uses:

(i) In contractions, to indicate that letters have been left out, *for example, can't, I'm, he's, you're* (you are).
Do not confuse: (a) 'you're' with 'your' (as in 'your hat');
                   (b) 'it's' (it is) with 'its' (as in 'The bird is on its nest').

(ii) To write the plural form of a word which does not normally have a plural form.
Examples: Children are confused by too many do's and dont's.
          You need to mind your p's and q's.
          Are there two m's in 'committee'?

(iii) To indicate the possessive case of a noun, *for example, Tom's book, the girls' signatures, the men's cars.*
(See also **Possessive forms of nouns**.)

35 Approve, Approve of

'Approve of' means 'regard favourably'; 'approve' means 'give permission for'.
*Examples: Do you **approve of** my choice of furnishings?*
          *My plans for building a workshop have been **approved** by the local council.*

36 As

(i) Use 'as ... as ... ' in positive statements; and 'so ... as ... ' in negative ones.
*Examples: A rhinoceros is **as** big **as** a hippopotamus.*
          *It is **not so** hot today **as** it was yesterday.*
However, 'as ... as ... ' is often used in expressing denials.
*Examples: He is **not as** foolish **as** we thought.*
          *You are **not as** ill **as** you pretend to be.*
The traditional distinction between 'as ... as ... ' and 'so ... as ... ' is now often ignored.

(ii) The term 'equally as' is incorrect. A thing may be '**as** cheap **as**' another; two things may be 'equally good', or 'equally cheap'.

(iii) Which pronoun, 'I' or 'me', is required in the sentence, 'He seems to like her as much as (I, me)'? The answer depends on the meaning, and the correct pronoun is indicated if the sense is written in full, *for example, as much as **I** do; as much as he likes **me**.*

(iv) In 'Tom is as tall or taller than Bill', 'as' is required after 'tall'. 'Tom is as tall **as** or taller than Bill', or preferably, 'Tom is as tall **as** Bill, or even taller'.

(For the use of 'as' and 'like', see **Like**.)

37 As far as, So far as

(i) When referring to distance, 'as far as' is used.
Example: He went as far as he could.
(ii) When distance is not referred to, 'as far as' is generally used, but 'so far as' is a possible alternative.
Examples: He is coming, as far as I know.
She is not an applicant, so far as I know.

38 As follows

This form is used in all cases, whether the related noun is singular or plural.
Example: The reasons given are as follows. (not *as follow*)

39 As from, As of

(i) The expression 'as from' should be used only when referring to a date in the past; 'as' is not necessary when referring to a future date.
Examples: The increased salaries will be paid as from the beginning of the present financial year.
The increased salaries will be paid from the beginning of the next financial year.
(ii) The confused term 'as of' should be eliminated.
Incorrect: All fares will be increased as of today.
Correct: All fares will be increased from today.

40 As to

This term is used correctly when 'to' introduces an infinitive.
Example: I am not so foolish as to play football with an injured knee.
It is used **wrongly** in the following sentences:
I will enquire as to whether accommodation is available here. (Omit 'as to': *I will enquire whether ...*)
Have you any information as to his recent activities? (Substitute 'about' or 'concerning': *... information about his recent activities.*)
The main dish was palatable, but as to the soup and the dessert ...! (Substitute 'as for': *... but as for the soup ...!*)

41 As well as

(i) In the sentence, 'The **teacher**, as well as the pupils, **was** amused by the circus animals', the subject is 'teacher', a singular noun requiring a singular verb. 'Pupils' is part of a parenthetic phrase, and is not co-ordinated with 'teacher'; therefore it does not influence the verb. In the sentence, 'The **pupils**, as well as the teacher, **were** interested in the science demonstration', there is a plural subject requiring a plural verb.

(ii) The form of a pronoun used after 'as well as' depends on whether the pronoun is a subject or an object.

Examples: *These changes will affect you as well as **me**.* (*These changes will affect **me**.* 'Me' is used because it is the object of 'will affect'.)

*You objected to his suggestion, as well as **I**.* ('I' is used because it is the subject of the verb 'objected'. *You, as well as **I**, objected.*)

(*a*) *You criticized him as well as **I**.* (Both you and I criticized him.)

(*b*) *You criticized him as well as **me**.* (You criticized both him and me.)

42 Awful, Awfully

'Awfully', 'terribly', 'frightfully', and 'horribly' are often misused in sentences which express no thought about terror, fright or horror.

Examples: *He was **awfully** pleased.*

*He is **terribly** clever.*

Similarly, 'awful', 'terrible', 'frightful' are often used wrongly and ineffectively, as in 'That's an **awful** book' or 'It was a **terrible** party'. The words are ineffective because they tell us nothing about the book or the party. It is not difficult to find more expressive adjectives and adverbs. Words such as 'terrible' should be reserved for things that are terrifying or alarming.

B

43 Back again

In 'Please come back again soon', 'again' is unnecessary and should be omitted.

44 Back of

This American term is not accepted as good English. 'Behind' and 'at the back of' are acceptable alternatives.

*Correct: The haystack was built **at the back of** the woolshed.*

*Incorrect: The haystack was built **back of** the woolshed.*

45 Barely

'Barely' is used with 'when'—not 'than'—in a sentence such as, ***Barely** had he leapt from the car **when** it burst into flames.*

The same thought can be expressed using the correlatives 'No sooner . . . than . . .'.

*Example: **No sooner** had he leapt from the car **than** it burst into flames.*

46 Because

The following sentences are **incorrect**:

(*a*) *The reason he is ill is because he ate too many cream cakes.*

(*b*) *Because he comes from a foreign country is no reason for being unfriendly to a person.*

(*c*) *Why he was absent was because he was ill.*

In each of these sentences, 'because' merely repeats the idea expressed in 'the reason' or 'why'. It is correct to say:

(*a*) *He is ill because . . . ; The reason for his illness is that he . . .*

(*b*) *The fact that a person comes from a foreign country is no reason for being unfriendly to him.*

(*c*) *He was absent because . . .*

47 Beg

Letter introductions such as, 'I beg to apply . . .', 'I beg to advise you . . .', or 'I beg to acknowledge . . .' are out-dated conventions which were always meaningless. There is no need to apologize for applying, advising or acknowledging. Use simple language such as,

21

'I received your letter . . .', 'In reply to your letter . . .', 'Thank you for your letter . . .', or 'I have to inform you . . .'.

48 Besides, Beside

(i) 'Besides' means 'in addition'; 'beside' means 'by the side of' or 'next to'.

*Examples: There were four passengers **besides** the driver.*

*John sat **beside** the driver.*

(ii) 'Besides' sometimes means 'also' or 'moreover'.

*Example: There is no point in trying to climb that cliff; **besides** it is too dangerous.*

49 Better, Best

The general rule requires 'better' to refer to two things, and 'best' to three or more things.

*Examples: This is the **better** specimen of the two.*

*This is the **best** specimen of the three.*

Common usage has established the use of best to refer to two in 'May the best team win'.

50 Between

(i) 'Between' is a preposition, and any pronoun that follows it should be in the object form, *for example, me, him, her, them.*

*Examples: Share these nuts between Tom and **him**.*

*Share these nuts between Jane and **her**.*

*Share these nuts between **him** and **me**.*

(ii) We choose between one thing **and** another, not **or** another.

*Example: For my prize I was able to choose **between** a silver plate **and** a crystal bowl.*

(iii) 'Between' is followed by a plural. It is incorrect to say, 'When planting lettuces leave a space of one foot between each plant'. Change this to 'a space of one foot between plants'. 'Each plant' is one thing, and there is no such position as between one thing.

(iv) Writers no longer insist on using 'between' only when referring to two things, and 'among' for more than two.

Examples: There is little difference between the three of them.

The three scouts sold two hundred tickets between them.

51 Bona fides, Bona-fide

'*Bona fides*' (Latin, 'good faith') is a singular noun.

*Example: Are you satisfied that his **bona fides** is beyond doubt?*

22

'*Bona-fide*' is usually used as an adjective meaning 'genuine' or 'in good faith'.
Example: Are you making **bona-fide** *enquiries or just being inquisitive?*

52 Both

(i) *I found the play both amusing, exciting, and thought-provoking.* This sentence is incorrect; 'both' should not be used when more than two terms or items are involved. To correct the sentence, omit 'both'.
(ii) 'both . . . and . . .' is followed by a plural verb.
Example: **Both** *Henry and John* **have** *passed their examinations.*
(iii) Care is needed in the placing of 'both'. It is wrongly placed in, 'He is **both** insolent to his parents and to his teachers'. This should be, 'He is insolent to **both** his parents and his teachers'.
(iv) A preposition or other word occurring after 'both' should be repeated after 'and', unless another word completes the sense.
Examples: The bridge is notable **both for** *its strength and* **for** *its simplicity of design.*
The police made a thorough search **both inside** *the house and* **in** *the adjoining buildings.*

53 Brackets

Parentheses, involving the use of brackets or dashes, should be used sparingly. Usually commas serve just as well. The use of brackets or dashes, and the excessive use of commas, often leads to the writing of complicated sentences in which the meaning is lost.
Often a parenthesis adds nothing to the meaning, and so is unnecessary.
Example: If I were a rich man (*which I am not*), *I would. . .*
It is better to write:
If I were a rich man, which I am not, I would. . .

54 Brothers

The term 'the brothers Smith' is old-fashioned; the form 'the Smith brothers' is more commonly used today. Similarly, 'sisters' is placed after the surname, *for example, the Russell sisters.*

55 Burned, Burnt

(i) When the adjective is required, use 'burnt', *for example,* **burnt** *trees,* **burnt** *grass.*
(ii) When a verb is required, either 'burnt' or 'burned' is correct. However:
(a) 'burnt' is preferred in the transitive sense, that is, when the verb

23

is followed by the name of the object burnt.

*Example: The match **burnt** his fingers.*

(b) 'burned' is preferred in the intransitive. The thing being burnt is not named.

*Example: The fire **burned** for several hours.*

(c) 'burned' is more common in the figurative sense.

*Example: The fire of ambition **burned** within him.*

56 But

(i) *It never rains but it pours.* This is an accepted idiomatic use of 'but'.

(ii) "I couldn't help but laugh" is a confused combination of two sentences. Say simply, "I couldn't help laughing".

C

57 Can, May

'Can' (past tense 'could') is used to express ability; and 'may' (past tense 'might') is used to express permission or possibility.

Examples: *"Mother,* **may** *I have a bun?"*

"Yes, Bill, if you **can** *reach the cake tin on the pantry shelf."*

"Dad, **may** *I use your car tonight?"*

"Yes, if you **can** *get it to start."*

He asked if he **might** *try the new machine.*

I **may** *go to the show if the weather is fine.*

I thought I **might** *go abroad last year, but I changed my mind.*

In formal writing, these rules should be observed. However, in spoken English the use of 'can' and 'could' to express permission is often acceptable.

Example: Billy asked if he **could** *have another bun.*

58 Capital letters

A. The common uses of capital letters are

(i) to begin a sentence;

(ii) to begin a quotation:

He said, "Come here".

(iii) for the principal words in titles of books, plays, etc.:

The Grapes of Wrath, The Merchant of Venice.

(iv) for names (proper nouns), for example, persons, places, pets, ships:

John Taylor, London, Amazon, Mount Everest, Niagara Falls, Lake Geneva, Lassie, Nelson's flagship, 'The Victory'.

(v) For important events and historical periods:

the Renaissance, the Middle Ages, the Peasants' Revolt.

(vi) in references to the deity:

We call Him the Almighty.

(vii) in names of institutions and specific titles:

the Chancellor of Cambridge University, the Archbishop of Canterbury.

(viii) for names of days and months (which are derived from proper names) and special days:

Thursday (from Thor), *March* (from Mars), *Good Friday*, *Boxing Day*.
Names of seasons do **not** have capitals.
(ix) for religions and nationalities:
Jewish, Hindu, Arab, Christian.
The capital is **not** used in 'christian name' or in 'negro'.
(x) Proper nouns and other words written with a capital retain the
capital in hyphenated forms:
anti-British, non-Christian, post-Renaissance.
B. Capital letters are **not** used in
(i) words derived from proper nouns but no longer closely associated
with the person or place:
*brussels sprouts, a limerick, plaster of paris, indian ink, cardigan,
sandwich, platonic friendship, pasteurize.*
(ii) title-words used in a general sense:
president, bishop, headmaster, chairman.
(iii) names of academic subjects unless they are mentioned as
specific subjects of a course or examination. Capitals are required for
languages.
A surveyor needs a knowledge of geometry.
*The main languages taught in schools are French, German and
Spanish.*
I passed Mathematics but failed Economic History.

59 Case

A. Case refers to the relation of a noun or pronoun to other words
in the same sentence.
(i) A noun or pronoun which is the **subject** of a verb is said to be in
the **nominative case**. It names the doer of the action.
Examples: ***He** hit Tom.*
 ***Tom** hit him.*
A noun or pronoun which is the **object** of a verb is in the **objective
case.**
*Examples: He hit **Tom.***
 *Tom hit **him.***
(ii) Case of pronouns. A noun takes the same form whether it is the
subject of a verb, or the object. But pronouns take different forms.
*Examples: I chased **him.***
 ***He** hit me.*
'I' in the subject becomes 'me' in the object; 'he' in the subject
becomes 'him' in the object.
B. Important points:
(i) The pronouns 'I', 'we', 'he', 'she', 'they', and 'who' are used

(a) as the **subject** of a verb: *He is ill.*
(b) as a **complement**: *It is he* . . .
(ii) The pronouns 'me', 'us', 'him', 'her', 'them', and 'whom' are used
(a) as the **object** of a verb: *The dog bit him.*
(b) after a preposition: *Tom sits near him.*
(iii) Possessive case—see **Possessive forms of nouns**.
C. Many errors are made in selecting the correct pronoun when the pronoun is used together with a noun or another pronoun. It is helpful to remember that if a pronoun can be used alone, it can also be used in a similar sentence in combination with a noun or another pronoun.

*Examples: I often go fishing. **Tom and I** often go fishing.*
*The dog chased **me**. The dog chased **Tom and me**.*
*Will you play with **him**? Will you play with **John and him**?*
*Sit with **her**. Sit with **me**. Sit with **her and me**.*

D. Other examples of the correct use of pronouns:
We girls often play hockey. (subject)
*It was **she** who broke the vase.* (subject form in the complement)
*I saw Jean and **her** at church.* (object)
*To **whom** are you writing?* (object form after the preposition 'to')

60 Cause

(i) It is wrong to say, 'The cause of the accident was due to the slippery wet road'. This use of both 'cause' and 'due to' is an unnecessary repetition. Say either 'The **cause of** the accident was the slippery wet road', or 'The accident **was caused by** . . .'
(ii) 'Cause' meaning 'reason for' is followed by 'of', as in 'The **cause of** the accident was . . .'. 'Cause' meaning 'justification' is followed by 'for', as in 'There is no **cause for** alarm'.

61 Check, Cheque

(*a*) *Will you **check** the accuracy of his story?*
(*b*) *Our regiment tried to **check** the advance of the enemy.*
These sentences illustrate the two most common meanings of 'check'. In (*a*) the simple verb 'check' should be preferred to 'check up on'. 'Cheque' is the accepted English spelling of the word denoting a money order on a bank.

62 Choice

One has a choice between one thing **and** another.
*Examples: You have a **choice between** electing our opponents who are*
*not to be trusted **and** electing my party which has a long*
record of responsible government.

27

*For your birthday present you may **choose between** a cycle
and an air gun.*

63 Chronic

I had a chronic headache last night. This is incorrect; 'chronic' means
'of long duration', and not 'severe' or 'painful'. A chronic illness is
one that persists for a long time.

64 Circumlocution

Circumlocution is saying things in a roundabout way, or in a 'long-
winded' style. This style is to be avoided. A simple, direct style is
much more effective in conveying ideas.

*Example: There are significant indications that the forthcoming period
of relaxation from our daily toil may be adversely affected
by lengthy periods of inclement climatic conditions.*

This could be written:

*There are signs that the holidays may be spoilt by bad
weather.*

65 Clause

A clause is a simple sentence. See **Sentences—Types.**

66 Cliché

A cliché is a printer's metal plate bearing a phrase, word or illustra-
tion which is to be printed over and over again. The word is also used
to denote a saying or a term which has been used so often that it has
lost much of its original force, *for example, conspicuous by his
absence, a bloated capitalist, up with the larks, at the psychological
moment, as cold as ice.*

A thoughtful writer seeks fresh images. However, one should not become
snobbish about clichés. Their over-use is to be avoided always, but some
are still appropriate, their meaning is usually clear, and they are 'friendly'
in conversation. Terms such as 'green with envy' and 'the rat race' are
useful in conversation. They are much less acceptable when a number of
them are used together.

67 Clue

*Correct: The detective says he found an important **clue** at the scene of
the crime.*

*Incorrect: I need fifty pounds, and I **haven't a clue** how I am going to get
it.* (Say, *I don't know...,* or *I haven't any idea...*)

28

68 Coherence

Sentences and paragraphs should be coherent. Each sentence should be clear, and should grow out of what precedes it and lead on to what follows. As a result there will be a quality of logic running through the paragraph.

Incoherence in writing begins in the sentence, and then 'infects' the paragraph. It is usually the result of failure to plan the development of the topic, and failure to think about the structure of the sentence about to be written. The clauses and phrases comprising the sentence come in almost haphazard order, reflecting the disorderly mind that produced them.

The following sentences have the defect of incoherence, and several such sentences will surely make an incoherent paragraph.

(a) *He is the kind of boy who if he doesn't get his own way and then he refuses to play with the others.*

(b) *It is my opinion that King Lear after reading most of Shakespeare's plays is the most pathetic character.*

(c) *The ranger stood with a few natives trying to drive a lion into an open space that had taken shelter in some bushes in a stream in order to take a photo.*

The paragraph following shows the same lack of thought before writing began.

(d) *I was getting cold and tired and the clock struck midnight. So I decided to go to bed, but then I remembered that I had to finish some algebra. So I decided to do that. But before that I made a cup of coffee. And then I set to work, having got a rug to keep me warm.*

The sentences and the paragraph given here as examples of incoherent writing should be compared with the coherent versions given in Exercise 18 on page 143.

69 Collect

One collects a number of things, such as stamps, coins, or antiques. One does not collect persons or a single item such as a parcel, a suit, or a book. *For example, dustmen **collect** rubbish, agents **collect** rents, scouts **collect** old newspapers.*

70 Collective nouns

(i) Most group collectives have plural forms (*for example, herd— herds, committee—committees*) which take plural verbs. A difficulty is presented by the fact that the singular form is treated as singular or plural according to the sense, and a singular or plural verb must be chosen accordingly.

29

If unity is stressed, a collective noun takes a singular verb; otherwise a singular or a plural verb may be more appropriate according to the sense.

Examples: (*a*) *The committee **was** unanimous in **its** decision.*

        (*b*) *The jury **has** retired to consider **its** verdict.*

        (*c*) *The congregation **were** requested to keep **their** seats.*
(Because we must refer to 'seats', a plural noun, and not the singular 'seat', we must write the rest of the sentence with a plural sense.)

But   (*d*) *Parliament **was** divided on the question of conscription.*
One thing *is* (past tense, *was*) divided.

        (*e*) *The jury are divided about the verdict.*
(Disunity rather than unity is stressed, and the plural is therefore more appropriate.)

(ii) A collective noun must be regarded as either singular or plural throughout a sentence.

The committee has given sound reasons for the change of plans, so we shall support their decision. This is incorrect. 'The committee has . . .' indicates a singular subject; therefore plural 'their' should be replaced by singular 'its' in 'support **its** decision'.

71 Colloquialisms

Between slang and standard English there is a level of language known as colloquial English. Colloquial language may be described as 'informal but not slovenly, correct but not formal'.

Examples of colloquial expressions are:

bats in his belfry;
a bee in his bonnet;
blowing his own trumpet;
in the black books;
a fit of the blues;
give him the cold shoulder;
backed the wrong horse;
flogging a dead horse;
a horse of another colour;
plenty of horse-sense;
a lot of horse-play;
riding the high horse.

The effective use of colloquialisms such as these requires restraint. When over-used they give the impression that the writer lacks an adequate vocabulary.

72 Colon

A colon marks a pause almost as long as that indicated by a full stop.

It is used to introduce a list, an explanation, a speech, a quotation, or a definition.

Examples: The bandit's voice was heard above the noise: "Stand back and you won't be hurt!"

He has studied the main branches of literature: fiction, biography, verse, and drama.

Wordsworth's sonnet begins:

'Earth has not anything to show more fair.'

73 Colossal

'Colossal' is one of the superlatives that are used far too much. In many cases a milder word would be more suitable. Other overworked superlatives are: *tremendous, fabulous, fantastic.* The excessive use of such words has two unfortunate effects: it gives an impression of insincerity, and it debases the meaning of the misused words so that when used correctly they fail to convey the meaning intended.

74 Comma

The following are the most common uses of the comma:

(i) To separate clauses, or to indicate places where a reader should pause.

Example: The Alps, the highest mountains in Europe, are snow-capped at all seasons.

(ii) To separate words or phrases in a series.

Example: The bandit fled across the street, up a lane, over a fence, and into a waiting car.

(iii) In letter writing, to mark off parts of headings and addresses.

(iv) To separate direct speech from the rest of the sentence.

Example: "I shall come," he said, "as soon as I can."

The excessive use of commas tends to confuse; use a comma only where it is required to clarify meaning and guide the reader.

75 Compare to, Compare with

(i) 'Compare to' is used when stating a resemblance between two things.

*Examples: Portia **compared** mercy **to** the gentle rain from heaven.*

*Shakespeare wrote, 'Shall I **compare** thee **to** a summer's day?'*

*Wordsworth **compared** Milton's soul **to** a guiding star.*

(ii) 'Compare with' is used when both similarities and differences are to be noted (usually with emphasis on the differences).

*Examples: Jones **compared** his car **with** mine to see who has the better bargain.*

*Most workers today are well educated **compared with** those of a century ago.*

31

76 Comparison of adjectives

(i) To compare things we use three degrees or levels of comparison;

(a) A quality is named by the **positive** degree, *for example, long, cheap, beautiful.*

(b) To compare two things, we use the **comparative** degree which denotes a higher degree of the quality.

*Examples: This is the **longer** rope of the two.*
*Jane is the **more beautiful** of the two sisters.*

(c) To compare more than two things the **superlative** degree is used. This denotes the highest degree of the quality.

*Examples: Is this the **cheapest** of the three brands?*
*I think Ann is the **most beautiful** girl in the group.*

(ii) All adjectives of more than two syllables, and some of two syllables, form the comparative and superlative by using the prefixes 'more' and 'most' respectively.

Examples: dangerous, more dangerous, most dangerous;
fertile, more fertile, most fertile

In some cases, the form used is a matter of personal preference.

Examples: lovelier or more lovely;
slenderer or more slender;
pleasantest or most pleasant

A few adjectives are compared in an irregular manner.

Examples: good, better, best;
many, more, most;
bad, worse, worst

(iii) Comparatives are modified by adverbs of degree such as 'much' or 'little', but should not be expressed as multiples.

*Correct: Iron is **much heavier** than aluminium.*

*Incorrect: Iron is **ten times heavier** than aluminium. (Say, ten times as heavy as . . .)*

(iv) Adjectives such as 'perfect', 'round', 'square', 'empty', 'full', 'right', 'wrong', or 'unique' have no comparative or superlative degrees. If a thing is perfect, round, empty, right, or full, another thing cannot be **more** perfect, **more** empty, etc. However, one thing can be **nearer** to perfection than another.

(v) It is incorrect to use double comparisons such as 'more louder', 'more fiercer', 'more neater'; in each case 'more' should be omitted.

77 Compliment, Complement

'Compliment' means 'an expression of praise'. 'Complement' means 'that which completes', or 'the full number'. 'Complement' is also a grammatical term. (See **Sentences—Types**.)

*Examples: He paid the girl a **compliment**.*
*The ship has its full **complement** and is ready to sail.*
*You should read this novel after that one; the second is **complementary** to the first.*
*In the sentence, 'Horses are quadrupeds', the **complement** completing the sentence is 'quadrupeds'.*

78 Comprise, Consist

'Comprise' should not be followed by 'of'.
*Examples: The flat **consisted of** a bedroom, a lounge and a kitchen.*
*The flat **comprised** a bedroom, a lounge and a kitchen.*

79 Concerned (about, with)

'Concerned about' means to be anxious about; 'concerned with' means to take part in (an activity).
*Examples: A doctor is concerned **with** the health of his patients.*
*A teacher is concerned **with** the education of his pupils.*
*A doctor would be concerned **about** a patient whose condition was growing worse.*
*A teacher should be concerned **about** a pupil who is making no progress.*

80 Concrete language. See Abstract language

81 Confide

We confide **in** a person, and confide information **to** a person.
*Examples: Jane often **confided in** her aunt.*
*Jane **confided to** her aunt that she had taken the purse.*

82 Confident, Confidant

'Confident' is an adjective. 'Confidant' is a noun meaning a person in whom confidence is placed.
*Examples: We are **confident** that we will win.*
*I am pleased that you regard me as a **confidant**.*

83 Confronted

The terms 'confronted by' and 'confronted with' are both correct, but each has its specific use.
(i) When immediate and perhaps dangerous opposition is involved, 'by' is the correct preposition.
*Examples: Suddenly we found ourselves confronted **by** an angry bull.*
*As the burglar turned away from the safe, he was confronted **by** a policeman.*

33

(ii) When the sense is that of coming face to face with a difficulty which does not involve an immediate threat, 'with' is used.
*Examples: I was confronted **with** an account for fifty pounds.*
*We were confronted **with** numerous difficulties.*

84 Congratulate

We congratulate a person **on** something such as a success, or good fortune.
*Example: Congratulations, Jane, **on** passing your exams!*

85 Conjunction

A. Conjunctions are joining words, used to connect words, phrases, or clauses (i.e. sentences). They have an important function in sentence structure. They also contribute to meaning; by changing a conjunction we can sometimes change the meaning of a sentence.
*Examples: You may have butter **and** honey on your bread.*
*You may have butter **or** honey on your bread.*
The most frequently used conjunctions are: *and, but, or, because, as, than, if, unless, although, where, when, before, after, until, while.*
B. Careless use of conjunctions can result in ambiguity. Consider the doubtful meaning of this sentence, the doubt being caused by the use together of the conjunction 'and' and commas.
I have to visit the dentist on Monday, Wednesday, and Friday next week. Does this sentence refer to three days next week, or to two days this week and one next week?
C. **Common errors in the use of conjunctions:**
(i) *Hold the ball **like** I showed you.*
(A conjunction is required here, and 'like' is not a conjunction. It should be replaced by the conjunction 'as'.)
(ii) *It looks **like** our visitors are arriving.*
('Like' should be replaced by 'as if'. Or, say 'Apparently our visitors . . .')
(iii) *John is as tall if not taller than Tom.*
(This sentence expresses two comparisons, but only one comparison is completed—'taller than'. The other comparison should be completed by the addition of the conjunction 'as': *John is as tall **as**, if not taller **than** Tom. John is **as** tall **as** Tom, if not taller.*)
(iv) *The reason why the peasants revolted was because they were living in misery.*
('Because' and 'reason why' express the same idea. Avoid this unnecessary repetition by saying, 'The reason why . . . was that they . . .' or simply, 'The peasants revolted because they . . .')

(v) *I'll come with you, providing you return in time for lunch.*
(Do not confuse the participle 'providing' with the compound conjunction 'provided that', which is required here—'provided that you return . . .')
(vi) *Please let us know (if, whether) you intend to visit us next week-end.*
(Which conjunction is required? 'If' suggests that advice is expected only if a visit is intended; 'whether' indicates that advice is expected whether a visit is intended or not.)
(vii) *Are you as tall as him? Yes, but he is heavier than me.*
(Both sentences are **incorrect**. After the comparative conjunctions, complete the sentence to find the correct pronoun:
. . . *as tall as he (is); . . . heavier than I (am).*
(viii) *This week-end I must mow the lawn; also I have to paint the toolshed.*
('Also' is an adverb, not a conjunction, and should not be used to join clauses. Say '. . . I must mow the lawn and paint the toolshed'.)
D. Some conjunctive words are used in pairs, and care should be taken to use the right combinations. (See separate sections.)
Examples: either . . . or;
  neither . . . nor;
  no sooner . . . than;
  scarcely . . . when;
  hardly . . . when;
  not only . . . but also

86 Consequent on. See Subsequent

87 Contact

This word is often used as a verb to refer to all or any methods of communicating with a person. It is more acceptable as a general term than as a substitute for a specific means of communication. We can justify saying, 'I must contact him by some means or other'. But we should not say, 'I decided to contact you', when we mean, 'I decided to write to you', or '. . . telephone you', or '. . . call on you'.

88 Contemptible, Contemptuous

'Contemptible' means 'worthy of contempt'; 'contemptuous' means 'showing contempt'.
*Examples: I think his action was **contemptible**.*
  *A politician cannot afford to be **contemptuous** of public opinion.*

35

89 Continuous, Continual

'Continuous' means 'going on without stopping'; 'continual' means 'going on almost without ceasing'.

Examples: **Continuous** *heavy rain has flooded the streams.*

I was kept awake by the **continual** *banging of a door.*

90 Correlatives

Correlatives are conjunctive words or expressions which always go together in pairs.

Examples: either . . . or;

neither . . . nor;

both . . . and;

not only . . . but also;

no sooner . . . than;

scarcely . . . when

Remember that these pairs **always** go together. 'A deaf mute can neither hear or speak', is wrong; 'neither . . . nor' is the correct combination. Say, '. . . can **neither** hear **nor** speak'.

Care should be taken to place correlatives correctly. Incorrect placing is seen in, 'You will **either** return my property immediately **or** I will start legal proceedings against you'. This should be: '**Either** you will return my property . . . **or** I will start legal proceedings . . .'

91 Covered (in, with, by)

(i) When 'covered' is used descriptively, to emphasize the sight rather than the action of the verb, 'in' may follow.

Example: His clothes were **covered in** *paint.*

(ii) When 'covered' is used as a participle (combining with an auxiliary or helper verb to form a complete verb) it is followed by 'with'.

Examples: The dining table was **covered with** *a hand-woven cloth.*

The sliced fruit should be **covered with** *water.*

(iii) When 'covered' means hidden, and the covering agent is named, the correct preposition is 'by'.

Example: The path around the deserted house was **covered by** *tall grass.*

92 Credible, Creditable, Credulous

'Credible' means 'worthy of belief'; 'creditable' means 'bringing credit'; 'credulous' means 'too ready to believe'.

Examples: The police concluded that his story was **credible**.

Winning a Rhodes scholarship is a **creditable** *achievement.*

Only a **credulous** *person would believe that the stars are electric lights.*

D

93 'Dangling' (unrelated) constructions

A 'dangling' or unrelated construction is a group of words which opens a sentence and is followed by a noun or pronoun to which the words do not refer.

(i) The unrelated **participle** (-ing) is a very common type of error.

Examples: *Reaching the top of the hill, the sea suddenly came into view.*

(The sea does not reach the top of the hill. Say, 'When we reached the top . . . the sea suddenly . . .')

Being a sunny day, we decided to walk along the beach.

('Being a sunny day' does not refer to 'we'. Say, 'As it was a sunny day, we decided . . .')

Having worked as a missionary for many years, my sympathy for the local people is deep.

(This makes the nonsensical statement that 'my sympathy' worked as a missionary. Say, 'Having worked . . . I have a deep sympathy for . . .')

(ii) The 'dangling' **infinitive** (to + verb) is another common error.

Example: *To swim well your heart and lungs must be strong.*

(Can your heart and lungs swim well? Say, 'To swim well you must have . . .')

(See also **Participles**)

94 Dash

The dash is used

(i) to mark a change of thought or an abrupt turn in the sentence, or to indicate faltering or interrupted speech.

Example: *"But you can't mean—Oh! Don't say you've changed your mind!" she cried.*

(ii) before and after a parenthetic remark.

Example: *Sometime in the 1580s—we cannot be sure of the date— Shakespeare must have arrived in London.*

(iii) to gather together a number of subjects.

Example: *Wives, daughters, sisters, mothers—all stood silent as the rescuers removed the fallen rock.*

37

95 Date

The word 'date' used instead of 'engagement' or 'appointment' is not recognized as good English.

96 Dates

(i) Dates are expressed in figures rather than in words, for example, 'in the year 1972' not 'nineteen seventy-two'; 'on November 5th' not 'the fifth'. However, when referring to a century words are preferred, for example, 'the nineteenth century' not '19th century'.

(ii) At the head of a letter '15 October, 1976' or '15th October, 1976' is preferred to 'October 15th, 1976', but all three are acceptable. Americans write the month first; thus 4/10/76 means April 10th, 1976.

(iii) A period of years is indicated in two ways: (a) *from 1927 to 1968;* or (b) *1927–68,* but not 'from 1927–68'.

(iv) When using the abbreviations B.C. and A.D., it is logical to write B.C. (before Christ) **after** the year, and A.D. (*anno Domini*, in the year of our Lord) **before** the year, *for example, 43 B.C.* and *A.D. 1066.*

97 Defective, Deficient

'Defective' suggests a defect, fault or flaw. 'Deficient' suggests a shortage, that is, something missing or lacking.

*Examples: This watch is **defective**; I shall return it to the watchmaker.*
*That building is a home for the mentally **deficient**.*
*His illness is caused by a **deficiency** of red corpuscles in the blood.*

98 Definitely

This is one of our overworked words. Often it is used unnecessarily, as in, 'John is definitely taller than Bill', and 'I am definitely going to be late for my appointment'.

It is correctly used in the two sentences following:

*The match is **definitely** arranged for 17th March.* (Perhaps after several dates had been suggested.)

*Are you **definitely** entering for the singles championship?* (Or have you not yet decided?)

99 Deny, Refute

'Deny' means 'state that something is false'; 'refute' means 'prove that a statement is false'.

*Examples: He **denies** that he betrayed your confidence.*
*He was able to **refute** the charge that he had betrayed his friend's confidence.*

100 Dependant, Dependent

'Dependant' is a noun.

*Examples: I am my father's only **dependant**.*
*A taxpayer can claim a deduction for every **dependant**.*

'Dependent' is an adjective.

*Examples: Children are **dependent** on their parents.*
*He is a very **dependent** person who does little to help himself.*

101 Desert, Dessert

*The explorer was lost in the **desert** (pronounced dés-ert).*
*We had fruit salad for **dessert** (dess-ért).*
*He has lived foolishly and now he has had his **deserts** (des-érts). (What he deserves.)*

102 Differ, Different

(i) 'Differ' is followed by the preposition 'from'.

*Example: On this subject my opinions **differ from** yours.*

(ii) 'Differ' is often used wrongly in place of 'vary'.

*Example: A person's opinions on some subjects may **vary** (not **differ**) according to the state of his health.*

(iii) Following on (i) it is logical to say 'different **from**' rather than 'different **to**'.

*Example: Prospects for our primary industries are very **different from** what they were a few years ago.*

'Different **to**' is less logical but is acceptable to many writers. 'Different than' is not acceptable.

(iv) 'Different' is not required in a sentence such as 'Three different bands played during the evening'. Three bands **must** be different; they could not be the same.

'Different' **is** required in the sentence, 'On the second night the play was presented by different performers'.

103 Direct, Indirect speech

A. (i) If we wish to report something that has been said, we can do so in two ways. We may

(a) choose our own words to give the **substance** of what was said. This is **indirect speech**.

Example: The teacher asked Tom why he was late. Tom explained that his bicycle chain had broken.

39

(b)   give the **exact words** that were used. This is **direct speech**.

Examples: The teacher asked "Why are you late, Tom?"
Tom replied "I apologize for being late. My bicycle
chain broke".

Note that the words quoted are enclosed within inverted commas.
Modern usage favours the use of single inverted commas for normal
quotations. (See also B. (iv) below.)

(ii)   When writing indirect speech take care to avoid the kind of ambiguity
found in this sentence.

Example: Ted told his brother that he had acted dishonestly.

Who acted dishonestly—Ted or his brother? The use of an appropriate
verb will clarify this point, *for example, Ted admitted . . . ,* or *Ted
accused . . .*

(iii)   When writing dialogue, devote a separate paragraph to the speech of
each speaker.

B.   There are certain rules for the punctuation of sentences in which direct
speech is quoted.

(i)   Punctuation stops are used inside inverted commas, unless the sense
dictates otherwise, as in Example (b). Note carefully the position of full
stops, question marks, exclamation mark and inverted commas in the
following sentences.

Examples: (a)   Mother said, "Take an umbrella, Jane, in case it rains."
(b)   Why did he shout, "You'll be sorry you said that!"?
(c)   The judge said, "Have you any evidence to support that
argument?"

(ii)   After a break, a quotation continues without a capital letter, unless a
new sentence is begun.

Examples: (a)   "I suspect foul play," said the detective, "and I think I
know who is responsible."
(b)   "I have planted the dahlias," said the gardener. "Have
you any other jobs for me this morning?"

In (b), the deciding factor in the use of a capital letter for 'Have' is that the
gardener's words form two separate sentences.

(iii)   It is recommended that double inverted commas be used to show
direct speech and single quotation marks to show a title which is referred
to or a quotation within a quotation.

Examples: The teacher said, "I want you to find the meaning of the
phrase 'noblesse oblige'."
The witness said, "Suddenly the accused shouted, 'Stand
back or I'll shoot!' and ran from the bank."
I said, "I'm going to see a performance of 'Macbeth'
tomorrow evening."

Note: The terms 'inverted commas' and 'speech marks' are both acceptable; it is often useful to refer to single marks as 'quotation marks' in order to distinguish them, but this practice is not universal.
(See also **Quotation marks**)

104 Discover, Invent
'Discover' means to bring to light something already existing.
'Invent' means to originate something, to devise something new.
*Examples: William Harvey **discovered** the facts concerning the circulation of the blood.*
*Alexander Bell, a Scottish-born Canadian, **invented** the telephone.*

105 Disgusted
We are disgusted **with** a person, and disgusted **at** or **with** a sight, a fact, or an event. Some writers also accept 'disgusted **by**' (a fact or event).

106 Disinterested, Uninterested
'Disinterested' means 'having no self-interest', or 'being impartial'.
'Uninterested' means 'not interested'.
*Examples: A judge should be **disinterested** in the cases which come before him.*
*It is difficult to pass exams if you are **uninterested** in your studies.*

107 Displace, Replace
'Displace' suggests dismissal or rejection; 'replace' suggests the filling of a position that becomes vacant.
*Examples: The elderly and frail watchman was **displaced** by a younger man.*
*When the secretary resigned he was **replaced** by a young accountant.*

108 Dissatisfied. See Unsatisfied

109 Distinct, Distinctive
'Distinct' means 'clear', 'obvious', or 'well-defined'. 'Distinctive' means 'characteristic of' or 'belonging to' a particular thing, making it different from anything else.

41

*Examples: Paint has a **distinctive** smell.*
*There was a **distinct** smell of petrol near the blazing building.*

110 Doctor, Dr

(i) The abbreviation, 'Dr' is used as part of a name.
Example: Dr Foster attended to the injured man.
(ii) When the word is used in place of the person's full name, it is written in full with a capital letter.
Example: Finally, I wish to thank the Doctor for his interesting lecture.
(iii) The form 'doctor', spelt without a capital letter, is used in a more general sense.
Examples: I think we should send for a doctor.
Michael hopes to become a doctor.

111 Double negative

(i) A double negative gives an affirmative meaning. Often this is not intended and is incorrect.
*Example: He says he **hasn't** had **no** lunch.* (The meaning intended is, '... he has had no lunch', or '... he hasn't had any lunch'.)
(ii) Sometimes two negatives are used intentionally and correctly to give an affirmative meaning.
*Examples: The punishment was **not** entirely **undeserved**.*
*His resignation was **not unexpected**.*

112 Doubt

The verb 'doubt' should be followed by 'whether', not by 'if'.
*Example: I doubt **whether** it will rain today.*

113 Drank, Drunk

The past tense of the verb 'to drink' is 'drank'.
*Example: The baby **drank** the milk quickly.*
'Drunk' is the past participle. This is used with auxiliary verbs, such as 'have', 'has', 'is', or 'was', to form verbs in sentences such as these.
*Examples: The baby **has drunk** its milk.*
*Wine **is drunk** by many southern Europeans.*
'Drunk' is also correct in, 'The wine (which was) **drunk** by the guests was the oldest available'.

114 Due to

(i) 'Due' is an adjective; therefore it should qualify a noun.

42

*Examples: This **mistake** is **due** to carelessness.*

*His **absence** was **due** to illness.*

***Accidents due** to carelessness are very common.*

*Engine **failure**, **due** to a block in a petrol pipe, caused an hour's delay.*

(ii) 'Due to' should not be used as a compound preposition meaning 'because of' and introducing a phrase of reason. This error is found in the following sentences. 'Owing to' or 'because of' should replace 'due to'.

Examples: Due to illness, I could not go to the football match.

There were several accidents, due to a dense fog.

Due to the big crowd watching the procession, we avoided the main streets.

A correct example of the use of 'owing to' is:

*The train was late **owing to** an accident on the line.*

(iii) If 'due to' is incorrectly used instead of 'owing to', as it often is, ambiguity may arise.

Examples: I did not wait after the accident due to my being in a hurry.

(Was my being in a hurry the cause of the accident, or was it the reason why I did not wait?)

I did not go to the conference due to the heat wave. (Was the conference due to the heat wave? Or was the heat wave the cause of my absence?)

E

115 Each

(i) *Each boy has his own locker.* In this sentence 'each' is an adjective. It qualifies the singular noun 'boy', and the singular subject, 'each boy', requires the singular verb 'has'. The pronoun used in place of 'boy' is singular 'his'.

If 'boy' is omitted from the sentence, 'each' remains as the subject and still requires a singular verb, *for example, Each has his own locker.* In this sentence 'each' is a singular pronoun.

(ii) When 'each' refers to two singular nouns, a plural verb is usually used, *for example, My brother and sister each give freely to charity.* But if it is intended to differentiate between the two singular nouns, a singular verb may be used, *for example, The tropical north and the arid interior of Australia each has its own agricultural problems.*

(iii) *Each of the girls has been presented with a bouquet.* In this sentence the true subject is 'each', and the verb agrees with 'each' rather than with 'girls'; therefore the verb is singular, 'has'.

Examples of other correct sentences:

Each graduate has received his diploma.

Each has been given his certificate.

Each of the contestants was awarded a medallion.

The Russians and the Chinese each claim part of Eastern Asia. (In this sentence 'each', referring to the Russians and the Chinese, is plural and takes the plural verb, 'claim'.)

116 Each other

(i) The rule that 'each other' refers to two, 'one another' to more than two, is no longer strictly followed. It is now acceptable to say, 'The three neighbours often helped each other with odd jobs'.

(ii) *The passengers waited for each other to leave the compartment.* This should be amended to: *Each passenger waited for the other(s) to leave* . . .

(iii) *Neither of the drivers saw each other.* This is clearly incorrect. Write: *Neither of the drivers saw the other.*

(iv) 'Each other' is reciprocal; 'one another' is not. Therefore 'one another' and not 'each other' should be used in the sentence, 'The

floats in the procession followed **one another** in quick succession'.
Each cannot follow the other, but one can follow another.

(v) In the possessive form, the apostrophe is always placed before
the 's', *for example, The twins often wore each other's clothes.*

117 Easy, Easily

'Easy' is an adjective; 'easily' is the equivalent adverb.
*Examples: These **exercises** are **easy**.*
*I can **do** these exercises **easily**.*
In certain idiomatic expressions, the adjective is used where we
would expect to find the adverb, *for example, go easy, take things easy,
easy-earned money* (cf. *hard-earned cash*).

118 Edible, Eatable

'Edible' refers to what can normally be eaten; 'eatable' to its
condition for eating.
*Examples: Apples and pears are **edible fruits**, but decayed apples and*
*pears may not be **eatable**.*
*A meat pie is **edible** but a burnt pie may not be **eatable**.*

119 Effect. See Affect

120 Effective, Efficient

These adjectives are similar in meaning, but are not always inter-
changeable.
'Effective' means 'having an impressive effect'.
*Examples: Hitler was an **effective** speaker.*
*This law becomes **effective** on the first of July.*
*This spray is very **effective** in killing aphids.*
'Efficient' is often applied to persons, but is also used in reference to
things such as machines.
*Examples: Miss Jones is an **efficient** secretary.*
*This business has prospered because of **efficient** manage-*
ment.
*The rotary car engine is a very **efficient** machine.*

121 Either of

(i) 'Either of' is used only of two things, and it always takes a
singular verb.
*Examples: **Either of** these presents **is** suitable.*
*If **either of** you **wishes** to go you may leave early.*

> *If **either** of them **applies** for the position, I shall withdraw my application.*
> ***Has either** of the two agents called?*

(ii) For more than two, use 'any one'.

*Example: **Has any one** of the three collectors returned yet?*

122 Either . . . or, Neither . . . nor

(i) 'Either' is followed by 'or', 'neither' by 'nor'. 'Either . . . or' and 'neither . . . nor' are used when referring to only two things. A singular verb or a plural verb is required according to whether the co-ordinated terms are singular or plural.

*Examples: Either Tom or James **has** already mended the gate.*
(Singular nouns, singular verb, 'has'.)
*Neither he nor she **has** been selected in the team.*
*Either the Browns or the Smiths **are** coming up the drive.*
(Plural nouns, plural verb, 'are'.)
*Neither the Thompsons nor the Grahams **have** accepted the invitation.*

(ii) If each term requires a different verb, use both forms of the verb as appropriate.

*Examples: Either **he is** or **I am** the winner.*
*Either **you are** or **he is** to blame.*

Sentences such as these are nearly always awkward. Often it is better to reframe the sentence, *for example, Either he is the winner, or I am.*

123 Eminent, Imminent

'Eminent' means 'famous', or 'distinguished'.

*Example: Many **eminent** scientists warn of the dangers of a polluted environment.*

'Imminent' means 'near at hand', 'impending', or 'threatening'.

*Example: Seeing that a storm was **imminent** we ran for cover.*

124 Enclosed

This word is involved in two common examples of commercial jargon.
(i) *Enclosed please find a cheque for twenty pounds.* This suggests a game which requires the receiver to search for the cheque. It is more sensible to say simply, 'I enclose a cheque . . .'
(ii) *Enclosed herewith . . .* These two words each say much the same thing. It is enough to say 'Enclosed is my cheque for ten pounds' or 'I enclose a cheque . . .'

125 Endure, Tolerate

'Tolerate' is often used when 'endure' is the meaning intended. 'Endure' suggests suffering, usually in silence; to 'tolerate' something means to allow it, with some degree of approval.

*Examples: He **endured** the pain without complaint.*
*Her company is something I cannot **endure** for long.*
*Our teacher will not **tolerate** laziness.*
The strange dog tolerated our presence but appeared restless and apprehensive.

126 Equally as well as

'As' means 'equally', so this phrase includes an unnecessary repetition. It is found in incorrect sentences such as, 'I can skate equally as well as he can'. This should be either 'I can skate as well as he can', or 'He and I can skate equally well'.

127 Especially, Specially

'Especially' means 'to an unusual degree'.
Example: We have had a number of especially heavy frosts.
'Specially' means 'for a special purpose'.
Examples: Mother baked this cake specially for you.
They won't change the regulations specially for you.

128 Euphemism

Generally, a direct statement is better than a euphemism, for example, 'died' is clearer and more acceptable than 'passed away' or 'departed this life'. Nevertheless, there are occasions on which the writer might feel that such an explicit statement would cause offence or pain, and courtesy would then suggest that a euphemism is preferable. Occasionally, euphemisms are accepted in official writing, for example, 'He was detained during Her Majesty's pleasure' means 'He was imprisoned'.

129 Euphony

(i) This term refers to pleasantness of sound in language. Many writers of poetry and prose are skilled in using the vowels and consonants, and words, to produce pleasant-sounding effects. Almost any volume of poetry will provide numerous examples.

(ii) Another approach, though negative, is also important—the avoidance of phrases which create ugly sounds or which produce unintended humorous effects, such as those found in the following examples:

47

The prompt action of the low-tax faction gave satisfaction to the whole population of the nation.
When the spy recovered he discovered that his undercover activities had been uncovered.
The children enjoyed the frantic antics of the clown.

130 Every

When 'every' is used before a noun, it should not be followed by a plural word such as 'they' or 'their'.

*Incorrect: Every reporter sent **their** stories with the least possible delay.*

*Correct: Every reporter sent **his** stories . . .*

131 Everyone, Every one, Everybody

(i) These pronouns are singular, and any words (for example, other pronouns) that refer to them should be singular.

*Examples: Everyone seems to have **his** (not **their**) own opinion on the subject. ('Everyone' is one word.)*
*Every one of these watches **is** (not **are**) faulty. ('Every one' is two words.)*

(ii) Sometimes, especially in colloquial language, 'everyone' and 'everybody' may be considered as plurals, referring to all the people in a given situation rather than to those people as individuals. The following sentences are accepted as good English:

*As smoke filled the corridors, **everybody** grabbed **their** belongings and fled for **their** lives.*
***Everybody** received a present, didn't **they**?*

132 Except, Excepting

(i) 'Except' is a preposition and is followed by the object form of pronoun: *me, us, him, her, them*.

*Example: The facts seem to be known by everybody **except me**.*

(ii) 'Except' (not 'excepting') is used to exclude individual persons or things from a general group or category.

*Example: All our soft fruits are ripe **except** the blackberries.*

(iii) 'Except for' is used to make a reservation modifying a general statement.

*Example: I have enjoyed perfect health, **except for** an occasional cold.*

(iv) 'Excepting' is often used (a) with 'not' to emphasize inclusion rather than exclusion, and (b) with 'always'.

*Examples: (a) Everyone present will be searched, **not excepting** the host and hostess.*

    (*b*) *In future, persons entering this area will be questioned,* **always excepting** *those who carry our identification cards.*

(v) Do not confuse 'except' with 'accept'.

Example: All the boys had spending money **except** *Tom; he would not* **accept** *any from his friends.*

133 Exclamation mark

A. This mark is used

(i) after an exclamation, *for example, Hurrah! Stop that! Good luck to him!*

(ii) to express ridicule or sarcasm, *for example, How clever you are!*

B. (i) Most writers use the exclamation mark at the end of a sentence only.

Example: Oh, how I wished you had been there!

(ii) Exclamation marks in quoted passages—see **Quotation marks**.

134 Exhausting, Exhaustive

'Exhausting' means 'causing exhaustion'; 'exhaustive' means 'thorough', or 'complete'.

Examples: After our **exhausting** *climb we rested at the top of the cliff.*
        An **exhaustive** *search was made for the cause of the damage.*

F

135 Fabulous

'Fabulous' originally meant 'as in a fable', but nowadays it is more often used to mean 'immense' or 'astonishing'. It should not be used carelessly to refer to things such as 'fabulous bargains' or 'a fabulous party'. It could be used to describe something 'almost unbelievable', such as a journey of adventure or a place of unusual beauty or opulence.

136 Face up to

This three-word phrase is often used when the word 'face' would be sufficient.
*Example: He will not **face** (up to) the facts.*
However, 'face up to' does sometimes give emphasis, as in an expression of determination, and then its use seems justifiable.
*Example: I realize now that I must **face up to** the consequences of my foolishness.*

137 Familiar to, Familiar with

'Familiar to' means 'known to'; 'familiar with' means 'having a knowledge of' or 'being on close terms with'.
*Examples: That face is **familiar** to me.*
*I am quite **familiar with** the roads in this area.*
*An officer should not become too **familiar with** the men he has to command.*

138 Fatal, Fateful

'Fatal' is often used loosely; it implies a death (fatality). It is usually a great exaggeration to say, 'You have made a **fatal** mistake'.
'Fateful' means 'affecting someone's fate'.
*Example: Today the government has to make a **fateful** decision concerning the nation's defence.*

139 Feasible

This word means 'practicable', 'able to be done'; it does not mean 'probable'. The following sentences illustrate correct and incorrect uses of the word.

Correct: *It doesn't seem **feasible** that men could live on Mars.*
        *The construction of a new bridge is **feasible**, but it will be an expensive project.*

Incorrect: *It seems quite **feasible** that snow will fall tonight.*
        *It is **feasible** that we may spend our holidays at the seaside this summer.*

140 Fewer, Less

As a general rule use 'fewer' for numbers, 'less' for amount, *for example, **less** money, **less** time, **less** trouble: **fewer** students, **fewer** cars, **fewer** attempts.*

*Examples: John eats **less** meat than Tom.*
        *Tom has **fewer** foreign stamps than John.*

Often it is possible to say the same thing in different ways.

*Example: There **were fewer** spectators than we expected.*
        *The crowd **was smaller** than we expected.*

(See also **Less**.)

141 Finalise

This over-used word is both unattractive and unnecessary. In most contexts 'complete' is a satisfactory alternative.

142 For ever

This should be written as two words except where the meaning is 'constantly', in which case either the one-word or the two-word form is acceptable.

*Examples: Your good luck will not go on **for ever**.*
        *He is **for ever** (or **forever**) grumbling about his rheumatism.*

143 Formal invitations

A formal invitation is written in the third person and is usually answered in the same style. In some cases, such as an invitation to the marriage of the daughter of a close friend, a less formal reply is appropriate.

Invitation:

Mr and Mrs John Brown request the pleasure of the company of Miss Mary Smith at the marriage of their daughter Anne to Mr William Jones, at St Margaret's Church, Ashville, on Saturday 5th September, 1975 at 2 p.m.

Reply:
Miss Mary Smith accepts with pleasure Mr and Mrs Brown's kind invitation to their daughter's marriage on 5th September, 1975.

144 Free of, Free from

To indicate the absence of some factor such as cost, or tax, or import duty, the term 'free of' is used, *for example,* **free of** *charge.*
'Free from' is used when the thing spoken of is of a menacing nature, *for example, pain, trouble, fear, starvation, worry.*

145 From, Off

These words do not mean the same thing. We take something **from** a person, and **off** an inanimate thing.
Examples: Please take those parcels **off** *the counter.*
I took the knife **from** *the child.*

146 -ful

(i) When 'full' is added to a noun to form a compound noun, one 'l' is dropped, *for example, cupful, spoonful, handful.*
Examples: **A bucket full** *of water stood at the entrance to the hut.* (two words)
The fireman threw **a bucketful** *of water on the smouldering papers.* (one word)
(ii) The plural forms are 'cupfuls', 'spoonfuls', and 'handfuls'.
Examples: Near the entrance were **six buckets full** *of water.* (two words)
The fireman threw **six bucketfuls** *of water on the flames.* (one word)
Note: in speech, the sound of the word might dictate a different plural. 'Cupfuls' is usual, but 'bucketsful' although technically incorrect, is often used as a more acceptable sound than 'bucketfuls'.

147 Full stop

(i) The full stop marks the longest pause in reading. It is used at the end of a sentence, unless it is a question or an exclamation, in which case a question mark or an exclamation mark takes the place of the full stop.
Examples: I'll see you tomorrow.
Where are you going?
What a foolish thing to do!
(ii) The full stop is used after initials and most abbreviations, *for example, R. M. Jones, B.A.; R. J. Smith & Co.; . . . at 7.45 p.m.*
(See also **Abbreviations**)

G

148 Gerund

(i) The gerund is similar in form to the present participle; both are part-verbs ending in '-ing', *for example, running, dancing, eating.* But the gerund is also part noun. It combines the functions of noun and verb by naming something and at the same time denoting an action.

Examples:
Present participle: *John was **swimming** in deep water.*
*Jane is **reading** a book of science fiction.*
Gerund: ***Swimming** is a healthy exercise.*
*Jane is fond of **reading**.*

(ii) When a pronoun or noun is used before a gerund, the possessive form is usually preferred.

Examples: (*a*) *I hope you will excuse **my** coming late.* ('**my**', not 'me')
(*b*) *The Smiths are not pleased about **John's** failing in his exams.*
(*c*) *There is little chance of **their** succeeding.* ('**their**', not 'them')
(*d*) *Do you approve of **his** being punished?* ('**his**', not 'him')

The possessive should not be used if it results in an awkward or ambiguous sentence. 'What is the likelihood of this flat being renovated?' is more natural than '. . . this flat's being renovated'.

149 Gold, Golden

'Gold' means 'made of gold', *for example, a **gold** ring, **gold** coins.* 'Golden' is now used only to speak of colour, *for example, a **golden** sunset, **golden** hair;* and in a figurative sense, *for example, silence is **golden**, a **golden** wedding.*

150 Got

(i) This word, like 'get', is used excessively by many people, and for that reason it has been almost banished from the language by some teachers. But it does have a place in our language; it is useful for emphasis, and is often acceptable in spoken English.

53

Examples: *We've **got** to win this match.* (This is more forceful than 'We **have** to win this match'.)

*I've **got** some really exciting news to tell you.* (This may be more natural than 'I have some really exciting news...')

*She **gets** on my nerves.* (This is acceptable colloquial English.)

(ii) It is not difficult to find more suitable verbs to replace 'got' and 'get' in sentences such as those that follow.

Examples: *He got drowned when his boat overturned.* ('**was** drowned')

Do you think he will get promoted soon? ('**be** promoted' or '**win** promotion')

I was glad when we got there. ('we **arrived**')

(iii) 'Gotten' is common in American English, but in standard English its use is restricted to one phrase, 'ill-gotten gains'.

151 Graceful, Gracious

'Graceful' refers to bearing or movement; 'gracious' denotes manner and disposition. A young ballet dancer could be described as 'graceful'; 'gracious' may be used to describe a person (in the sense of 'pleasant in manner') or a building (in the sense of 'agreeable in aspect'); it may also be used to suggest a slightly patronising attitude ('gracious towards inferiors').

152 Guess

The term 'I guess', meaning 'I think', 'I suppose', or 'I believe', is not accepted outside America by speakers and writers of good English.

H

153 Hackneyed phrases

There are many expressions that have been used so often that they have lost their force and have become tiresome.

*Examples: The secretary was **conspicuous by his absence**.*

*Mr Jones dined **not wisely but too well**.*

*His speech **struck a responsive chord in the hearts** of his audience.*

The use of hackneyed phrases is a sign of a tedious or insincere writer. It is always possible to express oneself in more appropriate and original language.

(See also **Clichés**)

154 Hanged, Hung

The form 'hanged' is used to refer to the hanging of a person; in other cases 'hung' is correct.

*Examples: The prisoner was sentenced to be **hanged**. He was **hanged** at sunrise next morning.*

*The portrait was **hung** above the fireplace.*

155 Hardly

When used as an adverb of degree, 'hardly' is followed by 'when'.

*Examples: He had **hardly** sat down to his meal **when** there was a loud knocking at the door.*

*We had **hardly** left the pier **when** a sudden gust overturned our yacht.*

An alternative expression is 'no sooner . . . than'.

*Example: We had **no sooner** left the pier **than** a sudden gust overturned our yacht.*

(See also **Correlatives**)

156 Has, Have

A verb must agree with its subject, which will be either a noun or a pronoun. Sometimes, when a verb is separated from its subject, it is easy to use a plural verb ('have' or 'are') where a singular verb ('has'

55

or 'is') is required, or vice versa. In each of the following correct sentences the related subject and verb are in bold type.

*The **manager**, as well as the employees, **has** made a donation.*

*The **pupils**, with the headmaster, **have** gone for a bushwalk.*

*There **have** been a few **cases** of measles.*

*He is one of those **who have** very poor prospects of success.* (The pronoun 'who' refers to the plural pronoun 'those', and takes the plural verb 'have'.)

*This is one of the most entertaining shows **that have** been seen here.* (The relative pronoun 'that' refers to the plural noun 'shows', and takes the plural verb 'have'.)

*A **pile** of boxes **has** been left on the platform.*

157 He, Him

In everyday speech, the expressions 'It's him' and 'It's me' are often heard, and are gaining acceptance. However, they are grammatically incorrect and should not be used, either in speaking or writing, in any but the most informal situations. The correct forms are 'It is I', 'It is she', and 'It is he'. The pronouns 'I', 'she', and 'he' are complements of 'is'.

(See also **Sentences—Types** and **Case**.)

158 Hereditary, Heredity

'Heredity' is a noun; 'hereditary' is an adjective.

*Examples: Which do you think has the greater influence on a person's character—**heredity** or environment?*

***Hereditary** diseases are passed on from parent to child.*

159 Him, His

When a pronoun is used before a gerund (a verbal-noun, such as 'coming', 'going', or 'laughing') the possessive form, 'his', 'my', 'your', or 'their', is preferred.

*Example: Tom's parents do not approve of **his** driving in car trials.*

(See also **Gerund**.)

160 His or her

*Every boy and girl is expected to play **his or her** part in making this show a success.* This sentence is awkward, but it is correct. Often it is better to recast a sentence to avoid an awkward construction: *Every boy and girl is expected to contribute something to make this show a success.*

Often, 'his' is used when distinction of gender is not important.
Example: **Each member** *should sign* **his** *own application.*
'His or her' is usually preferable, unless it results in an awkward or cumbersome sentence.

161 Historical, Historic

'Historical' may mean either 'concerned with history' (*for example, a* **historical** *novel*), or 'having actually existed in history' (*for example, Was King Arthur a* **historical** *character, or a mythical one?*)
'Historic' means 'having a long and important history' (*for example, a* **historic** *city or castle*), or 'sufficiently important to be recorded in history' (*for example, I think this will prove to be a* **historic** *occasion*). (See also **A, An.**)

162 Homonyms

(i) Homonyms are words which are pronounced alike but are different in meaning. Many spelling errors are caused by confusion over these words.

Examples: **Practice** *makes perfect. You should* **practise** *for two hours every day.*

The whole **populace** *rejoiced in the streets.* **Populous** *areas, such as New York, have many traffic problems.*

The racehorse ran off the **course.** *This sugar is very* **coarse.**

(ii) The following homonyms and near-homonyms are often confused. Refer to a dictionary to find the meanings of any of these words that confuse you.

horde, hoard; sight, site, cite; meter, metre; vain, vein, vane; illusion, allusion; sore, saw, soar; censer, censor, censure; weather, whether; chord, cord; serial, cereal; idle, idol; sole, soul; curb, kerb; threw, through; draft, draught; stake, steak; dying, dyeing; currant, current; peace, piece; break, brake; adapt, adopt; desert, dessert; persecute, prosecute; human, humane; past, passed; illegible, eligible; vacation, vocation; insulate, isolate; presence, presents; exceed, accede; recent, resent; bare, bear; descent, decent.

Note: Some authorities classify these word-pairs as **homophones** (Greek *homos*, the same; *phone*, sound) and confine the term **homonyms** to words which happen to be identical in form, for example, 'post' (*gate* **post, post** *a letter*); 'host' (*a* **host** *of golden daffodils, our* **host** *for the evening*).

163 Hyphen

A. The hyphen is used to link syllables and words which are thereby given a closer relationship. It should not be confused with the dash, which is used to indicate an interruption or abrupt change.

Compound words that are long established are usually written without the hyphen, *for example, today, teaspoon, headmaster, waterfall, windmill, baseball, wallpaper, greyhound.* However, this rule is not universally followed; many well-established compounds are written with a hyphen, *for example, non-Christian, ex-convict, son-in-law, post-war, twenty-one, second-rate.*

B. The hyphen is useful to

(i) clarify the meaning of words, *for example, recount, re-count; reform, re-form; green house, green-house; recover, re-cover; forty five-pound notes, forty-five pound notes.*

(ii) avoid awkward duplication of letters, *for example, co-operate, re-employ.*

(iii) combine two or more words as an adjective, *for example, an ice-cold drink, a take-it-or-leave-it attitude, a half-empty can, an up-to-date edition.* When the use is not adjectival no hyphens are used, *for example,* **Up to date** *we have received twenty applications.*

(iv) indicate a broken word at the end of a line. The break should be made at the end of a syllable, for example, 'employment', written 'employ-' followed by 'ment' on the next line.

I

164 Idiom

An idiom is an expression which is peculiar to a language.

*Examples: Everything was **spic and span**.*

*We must **keep our noses to the grindstone**.*

*You must **face the music**.*

*He was **given up for lost**.*

*This is **a pretty kettle of fish**.*

*The box was full of **odds and ends**.* (never 'ends and odds')

Some idioms break the rules of grammar but are still accepted as correct.

Examples: His words ring true. ('Truly' would be more correct.)

I nearly died with laughter. (One usually dies **of** something.)

As we grow up we become familiar with the idioms of our language. But to foreigners they are confusing and often incomprehensible. Imagine the difficulties of an immigrant trying to understand what we mean when we speak of 'a **sharp** knife', 'a **sharp** lad', 'a **sharp** tongue', 'a **sharp** taste', 'eight o'clock **sharp**', 'a **sharp** shower', 'a **sharp** note', or 'a card-**sharp**'.

165 If and when

The term 'if and when' is nearly always unnecessary and meaningless; it should be used only in special circumstances. In most cases either 'if' or 'when' is sufficient.

*Examples: I shall buy a new car **if** I win promotion.*

*I shall buy a new car **when** I win promotion.*

166 If, Whether

In some sentences 'if' or 'whether' can be used without fear of misunderstanding.

*Examples: Do you know **if** the manager is in?*

*Do you know **whether** the manager is in?*

In other sentences care must be taken to avoid ambiguity. For example, the sentence, 'Please let me know if you want a ticket for

59

the concert' could be understood to mean either (*a*) *advise me only if you wish to go to the concert*, or (*b*) *let me know in any case, whether you want a ticket or not*.

These two possible meanings are clarified in the following sentences:

(*a*) *If you require a ticket for the concert, please let me know*.

(*b*) *Please let me know whether you want a ticket for the concert*.

167 Imaginative, Imaginary

'Imaginative' means 'showing a good deal of imagination'.

Example: Edgar Allan Poe wrote many imaginative stories.

'Imaginary', means 'existing only in the imagination, not in reality'.

Example: Gulliver's Travels *is a story about imaginary lands where giants and dwarfs live.*

168 Imply, Infer

'Imply' means 'suggest or hint'; 'infer' means 'draw conclusions from a statement'. In a statement a politician could **imply** more than he actually says. From his statement a student of politics might **infer** certain things that were not clearly stated.

*Examples: When I said you were impetuous I did not mean to **imply** that you were foolish.*

*When I said he was impetuous he **inferred** that I considered him foolish.*

169 In, At

We speak of a person living **in** a country, **in** a city or large town, **at** or **in** a village, **in** a street, **at** a given address, working **in** a shop or kind of business house (*for example, in a bank*), **at** a specified establishment (*for example, at the Museum*).

170 Industrious, Industrial

A hard-working person is **industrious**. A city with many industries is an **industrial** centre.

171 Infinitive

An infinitive names an action in a general way. In modern English the infinitive usually consists of 'to + verb', *for example, to run, to hear, to think*.

However, the word 'to' is no longer an essential part of the infinitive, and it is sometimes omitted.

*Examples: I helped him **change** (to change) the flat tyre.*

*I have known him **laugh** (to laugh) at nothing.*

*They made me **leave*** (to leave) *the room.*
*We let him **go*** (to go) *back to his friends.*
*We saw him **enter*** (to enter) *the empty house.*
(See also **Split infinitive**.)

172 Inflammable, Inflammatory

'Inflammable' means 'easily set on fire'.
*Example: Petrol is one of the most **inflammable** liquids.*
In this word the prefix 'in-' means 'in', suggesting the meaning 'in flames'. This meaning of the prefix is also seen in 'inflationary', 'infectious', and 'influential'. However the prefix 'in-' has a second meaning, 'not', as in 'incorrect', 'invisible', 'inexpensive', and by analogy the word 'inflammable' may suggest the meaning '**not** easily set on fire'. Because of this possible confusion the word '**flammable**' is now widely used to describe something which readily catches fire.
'Inflammatory' means 'tending to cause something to burst into flames'. This word is often used in a metaphorical sense.
*Example: His **inflammatory** remarks soon stirred a rebellious mood among the crowd.*

173 Inflicted, Afflicted

Something unpleasant such as punishment is **inflicted** on a person. A person is **afflicted** with a disability such as rheumatism or deafness.

174 In receipt of

'I am in receipt of your letter . . .' is an abstract expression that was once popular in business circles. Nowadays most letter writers prefer a more direct opening, *for example*, *I have received your letter . . .*

175 Inst. Ult. Prox.

These are the abbreviated forms of the Latin words, '*instant*' (the present month), '*ultimo*' (last month), and '*proximo*' (next month). Most writers of business letters now prefer to write the name of the month.

176 Intense, Intensive

Although these words are similar in meaning they are not interchangeable. We speak of **intense** pain, **intense** excitement, **intense** concentration. (The meaning of intense here is 'to a high degree'.) But thorough, detailed study of a book is **intensive** study, and some farming which involves high yield from a small area is called **intensive** agriculture. (The meaning of 'intensive' here is 'concentrated', especially when directed to a particular limited aim, object or area.)

61

177 Interjection

An interjection is a word which is included in a sentence to express emotion, or to attract attention. It is followed by an exclamation mark.

Examples: **Oh!** *I have lost my watch.* (surprise, disappointment, dismay)

        Hurrah! *We have won the match.* (elation)

        Ouch! *Get off my foot!* (pain)

Some interjections cannot be accurately represented in written language, but are suggested by combinations of letters, *for example,* *Pshaw! Ugh! Huh!*

178 In the event of

In the event of your not being able to play . . . This is expressed more naturally if we say simply, 'If you are unable to play . . . .'

179 Intolerable, Intolerant

'Intolerant' refers to a narrowminded attitude or the language which expresses such an attitude.

'Intolerable' means 'unable to be tolerated or endured'.

*Examples: He is **intolerant** of all who are different from himself, whether by race or religion.*

        *Most people would find solitary confinement **intolerable**.*

180 Invaluable

In certain words the prefix 'in' means 'not', *for example, inconsistent, inflexible, inaccurate.* But 'invaluable' does not mean 'not valuable'. Its meaning is 'not able to be valued' or 'very valuable'. Note also 'inestimable' (not able to be estimated), and 'infamous' (famous, but for unworthy reasons, or notorious).

(See also **Inflammable**.)

181 Inverted commas, or Quotation marks

(See **Quotation marks** and **Direct Speech**.)

182 Its, It's

'Its' is a possessive; it has no apostrophe. 'It's' is a short form of 'it is' or 'it has'.

*Example: The cat has eaten **its** meat; now **it's** lying on the mat.*

Note that the possessives 'hers', 'yours', and 'theirs' also have no apostrophe.

*Example: My watch is broken; I hope to borrow **yours** or **hers**.*

183 It's me

Although it is grammatically incorrect, this term is widely accepted in everyday conversation. The correct form, 'It is I', is considered by some people to be too pompous for everyday use, but it should be used in any but the most informal writing. Similarly, 'It's him' and 'It's her' are more acceptable in informal speech. There is no affectation in using the simple, correct forms 'It is I', 'It is he', 'It is she'.

J

184 Jargon, Journalese

These two words refer to faults of style which every writer should strive to avoid.

A. **Jargon** may be defined as 'unintelligible words, gibberish, or speech full of unfamiliar terms'. It is found in two forms: firstly, as the special vocabulary of a sporting circle, social or occupational group writing for fellow members, and secondly, in more general use as unnecessarily complicated and verbose writing, which may appear impressive and mean little.

The first usage is acceptable as long as the writer or speaker can be sure that his audience will understand.

Example: (a sports writer, of a cricket match)
He tried to sneak a short single and was out for a duck.

The second usage is not acceptable as good style and should be avoided.

Example: At this present moment in time, it is essential to de-escalate the traffic density situations. (meaning 'There must be fewer vehicles on the road.')

C. **Journalese** is a hackneyed style which sometimes combines with flowery or pompous language and produces a ludicrous effect. Only mediocre writers use language that is so much overworked that it is no longer effective.

*Examples: Saturday's games were **marred by unfavourable climatic conditions.***
***To make confusion worse confounded,** it began to rain.*
*Several members were **conspicuous by their absence.***

(See also **Cliché**.)

185 Judicial, Judicious

Both words are adjectives, and both contain the idea of judgement, but they are used in different contexts. The use of 'judicial' is limited to legal matters and court proceedings. 'Judicious', meaning 'showing good judgement, discretion or discernment', is applied more widely to the affairs of life.

Examples: *We need to look at the claims with **judicial** impartiality.*
*There will be a **judicial** investigation following these charges of corruption.*
*His tactless comment was followed by a **judicious** silence.*
*The librarian made a **judicious** selection from the many books available.*

K

186 Kind (sort)

(i) 'Kind' is a singular noun and should be used in association with a singular adjective. Therefore, we should say 'This kind (sort) of . . .' or 'That kind of . . .', and not 'These kind . . .' or 'Those kind . . .' The plural forms are 'These kinds (sorts) . . .' and 'Those kinds . . .'.

Examples: **That kind** *of person annoys me.*

This kind *of apple is too sour for me.*

These kinds *of flowers are grown in the tropics.*

As an alternative the sentence can be reframed, for example, 'People like that annoy me.'

(ii) Either the singular or the plural noun may be used after 'What kind (sort) of . . .'

Examples: *What* **kind** *of bird is that?*

What **kind** *of berries are those?*

What **kind** *of nuts do you like?*

(iii) 'What kind of engineer is he?' is a question about a man's profession. Is he a mechanical engineer, an electrical engineer, a civil engineer, or some other kind of engineer?

'What kind of **an** engineer is he?' is a question concerning his efficiency.

L

187 Lack

'Lack' means an absence or shortage of something that is desirable—such as food, interest, time, money for a project, experience, foresight, intelligence or confidence. We would refer to the **absence** (not lack) of nervousness, selfishness, or conceit.

188 Latter

(i) When the term 'the latter' is used it should clearly refer to the second of two things mentioned previously. 'The former' refers to the first of two things mentioned.
Example: She offered us gifts of sweets or fruit; I chose **the latter**.
(ii) If more than two things are mentioned, 'the last' or 'the last mentioned' should be used. As an alternative the appropriate noun may be repeated.
Example: Apples, oranges and peaches were available; I bought some peaches.
(iii) There is no need to use 'the latter' when the sense is clear without it.
Example: After the class, the teacher spent some time talking to three students. **The latter** *were worried about their examinations.*
'The latter' is necessary; '. . . students who were worried . . .' would be perfectly clear.

189 Lay, Lie, Laid

The verb 'to lay' (set down) is transitive—that is, it names an action which passes over from a subject or doer, to an object. *For example, hens* **lay** *eggs, workmen* **lay** *drainpipes, builders* **lay** *bricks.*
The verb 'to lie' (stretch out) is intransitive; the action does not pass over to an object.
The following sentences show the correct use of the most common forms of the verbs 'to lie' and 'to lay'.

67

	Present tense	Past tense	Present participle	Past participle
to lie (stretch out)	*I **lie** in the sun. Baby **lies** in her pram. **Lie** down, Rover.*	*John **lay** in bed till he was called. We **lay** on the sand till lunch was ready.*	*The cat is **lying** on the mat. Baby is **lying** on the rug.*	*Mother has just **lain** down to rest. That log has **lain** there for years.*
to lay (set down)	*Hens **lay** eggs. Furnishers **lay** carpets. Plumbers **lay** pipes.*	*Our hens **laid** six eggs yesterday. He **laid** the books on the desk.*	*Our hens are **laying** well. The men are **laying** pipes in the drain. The builder is **laying** bricks.*	*Our canary has **laid** an egg. The men have **laid** the first row of bricks.*

190 Learn, Teach

A pupil learns; the instructor teaches.
*Example: I will **teach** you to drive; I am sure you will **learn** quickly.*

191 Lend, Loan

'Lend' is a verb; we **lend** things to our friends.
'Loan' is a noun; people get **loans** from banks to buy cars and houses.
*Example: If he asks for the **loan** of my mower, I will **lend** it to him.*

192 Less

(i) The general rule is to use 'less' for things measured by quantity, *for example, **less money**, **less time**, **less bread**, and 'fewer' for things measured by number, *for example, **fewer cars**, **fewer inquiries**, **fewer applicants**.
(ii) When a noun is already preceded by a numeral—such as 'few', 'many', 'several'—'less' is sometimes preferred to 'fewer' to indicate number.
*Example: We have **a few less** cows milking this year.* ('A few less' is better than the awkward phrase 'a few fewer'.)
(iii) *We raised ninety-eight pounds—only **two less** than our target.* 'Two less' seems more natural here than 'two fewer'.

193 Liable

(i) 'Liable' means 'obliged, responsible, or bound by law'. It can be used to refer to characteristics or actions which are the consequence of an inborn quality or of some condition over which the **person has little control**.

*Examples: All human beings are **liable** to make mistakes.*

*Is the tenant **liable** for repairs to fences?*

(ii) 'Liable' is often used where 'apt' or 'likely' is more appropriate.

Example: In August we are liable to have hot weather. (This should be '. . . we are **likely** to have hot weather'.)

When a person **chooses** to act in a certain way, 'apt' or 'likely' should be used rather than 'liable'.

*Examples: If you contradict him he is **apt** to lose his temper and become abusive.*

*He is **likely** to misunderstand if you act as you intend to.*

194 Licence, License. See **Advice, Advise**

195 Like

(i) *She is impatient, like him and me.* In this sentence 'like' is a preposition, and the pronouns that follow must be in the object form, 'him' (not the subject form 'he') and 'me' (not the subject form 'I').

(ii) *Tie the knots **as** (not 'like') I showed you.*

*Arrange the furniture **as** (not 'like') it was when we came.*

In these sentences, the conjunction 'as', and not the preposition 'like', is required to introduce adverb clauses.

(iii) *It looks like we are late.* This is not accepted as good English. Use another construction such as 'It appears that . . .'

196 Locate

'To locate' means 'to place' or 'to situate'; it does not mean 'to find'.

*Correct: Industries are usually **located** as near to the market as possible.*

*Incorrect: The golfer searched for an hour before **locating** his ball.*

197 Lose, Loose

'Lose' is the opposite of 'find'; 'loose' is the opposite of 'tight'.

198 Luxuriant, Luxurious

'Luxuriant' means growing in profusion'.

*Example: Plant life is **luxuriant** in tropical forests.*

'Luxurious' means providing luxury or great comfort'.

*Examples: I sank into the **luxurious** chair.*

*His **luxurious** manner of living is very costly.*

At present 'luxury' is a vogue word, used to excess as an adjective in phrases such as, 'a **luxury** liner', 'a **luxury** cruise', 'a **luxury** holiday', 'a **luxury** motel', '**luxury** furnishings'.

M

199 Manners

*Good manners **is** a desirable quality.*

*It **is** bad manners to serve yourself first.*

In these sentences 'manners' (meaning the quality of social conduct) takes a singular verb. Compare this with two other nouns ending in '-s': 'news' and 'mathematics'.

*Examples: No news **is** good news.*

*The news **is** disturbing.*

*Mathematics **is** my favourite subject.*

In some other sentences the plural verb is required.

*Examples: His manners **are** in need of improvement.*

*The total exceeds a million, if my mathematics **are** correct.*

200 May, Might

(i) 'Might' is the past tense of 'may'. 'May' should be used only as the present tense.

*Example: I'll take my coat; it **may** rain before I return home.*

(Although this sentence expresses the possibility of a future event, it is really a present estimate regarding the future.)

(ii) Use 'might' for the past tense.

*Example: We thought it **might** rain, so we took our raincoats.*

(iii) *They **may** have had car trouble.* This is a guess in the present about a possibility that still exists; therefore use the present tense 'may'.

(iv) *They **might** have all been killed.* This refers to a possibility that existed in the past, but exists no longer; therefore use past tense, 'might'.

Note: The distinction between 'may' and 'might' is becoming less clear, and the two forms are often confused in colloquial English.

201 Maybe

Some authorities object to the use of 'maybe' (one word) as a synonym for 'perhaps', but the word is widely accepted in friendly communication. In formal expression it is better to use 'perhaps'.

202 Me

'Who is there?' 'It's me.' 'It's me' is so widely used that it must be

regarded as an accepted idiom. However, in formal expression, and particularly when the sense continues in a longer sentence, the grammatically correct form, 'It is I' should be used.
Example: **It is I** *who am responsible for this misunderstanding.*

203 Melted, Molten

'Melted' is the past tense and also the part participle of the verb 'to melt'; it is used as a verb or part-verb.
*Examples: The snow **melted** quickly in the warm sunlight.*
*The snow **has melted** early this spring.*
'Melted' and 'molten' are both used as adjectives, the latter being restricted to things that are normally solid and hard, *for example,* **molten** *steel,* **molten** *metal,* **molten** *wax,* but **melted** *butter,* **melted** *snow and hailstones.*

204 Menace

This word is often used carelessly as a synonym for 'nuisance'. Its proper meaning is 'a threat'.
Correct: *We knew that falling rock would be the chief **menace** we would have to face.*
Incorrect: *Young Dennis is a real **menace**.*

205 Metaphor

In a metaphor a word is substituted for or associated with another to suggest a comparison.
Examples: **Sir Galahad** *was a **lion** in battle.*
*The government's action brought a **storm of protest**.*
A writer who begins a metaphor must be careful to complete it correctly and not confuse it with another. If a metaphor is 'mixed', it produces a humorous effect that is not intended.
*Examples: He set a trap for me, but I **smelt a rat** and managed to*
nip it in the bud.
*The road has been long and hard, and we've had to **change**
horses midstream, but we have finally **steered the ship of**
state safely to harbour.*

206 Mood

The term 'mood' refers to the manner in which a verb is used. A verb can be used
(i) to make a statement or ask a question; this is the **indicative** mood.
*Examples: The bus **arrived** on time.*
*Why **did** he **hit** you?*

71

In these sentences the verbs 'arrived' and 'did hit' are in the indicative mood.

(ii) to give a command or make a request; this is the **imperative** mood of the verb.

Examples: **Come** *here!*

            Please **help** *me.*

(iii) to express a wish, condition, exhortation, or hypothesis, in a verb form other than the indicative. This is the **subjunctive** mood. It is used in certain idiomatic expressions.

Examples: *If I* **were** *king, I would rule justly.*

            I wish he **were** *here now.*

            Though all care **be** *taken, mistakes will occur.*

            I move that Mr Jones **be** *appointed Treasurer.*

            I move that the meeting now **adjourn.**

            Be *that as it may, you will find that he is right.*

            We demand that the truth **be** *made known.*

            He spoke and acted as if he **were** *hypnotised.*

207 Mr, Mrs

(i) These abbreviations are formed by dropping part of the middle of the word while retaining the first and last letters, and therefore a full stop is not required after them.

(See also **Abbreviations**.)

(ii) The plural forms of the words are: **Messrs** Thompson and Jones; **Mesdames** Wright and Smith.

208 Much

Adjectives and adverbs may be modified by 'very', *for example,* **very** *slow,* **very** *slowly,* **very** *neat,* **very** *neatly.*

'Much' may be used to modify past participles, *for example,* **much-discussed** *problem,* **much-travelled** *man,* **much-maligned** *politician,* unless the participle has come to be recognized as strongly adjectival in function, *for example,* **very** *interested,* **very** *determined.*

209 Myself

The use of this emphasizing pronoun is justified in, 'I saw the incident **myself**, so I can give an accurate account of it'. But it is unnecessary and pointless in, 'I think **myself** that the pedestrian caused the accident'.

N

210 Neither

(i) 'Neither' is used where only two things are concerned.
'Neither of the three cars . . .' is incorrect; say 'None of the three cars . . .'.

(ii) 'Neither' refers to each of two things separately; therefore it takes a singular verb.

*Example: Both John and Ted are coming, but **neither has** arrived yet.*

(iii) For neither . . . nor, see **Correlatives**.

211 Neologism

A neologism is a new word that has recently come into use. There are fashions in words and sometimes older words come back into vogue, but these are not neologisms. Examples of words that have come into use in recent years are: *beatnik, disc-jockey, junkie.*

When a new word comes into use, it is interesting to consider this word's chances of surviving. Is the word necessary, or at least useful? Does the word suit the idea with which it is associated? Is the word attractive, or expressive?

Several of the examples given above have already survived for some years. Words such as *teenager* or *jet* (plane) have become part of the language, while recent (1980) neologisms, such as *lookalike*, may or may not last.

Are there obvious or probable reasons for the acceptance or rejection of neologisms?

212 Never

'Never' means 'at no time', so it is absurd to say, 'I never went to the football match last Saturday'. One says, 'I have **never gone** to the football match', that is, never on any occasion; or '**I didn't go** to the football match last Saturday'.

213 Nice

'Nice' is such a useful word that we use it far too often. When we speak of 'a nice day' or 'a nice meal' we mean that these things are pleasant or enjoyable, and there is little doubt that we shall continue to use 'nice' in this sense in spite of objections. There is less justification for speaking of 'a nice book' or 'a nice man'; we should be more precise, *for example, an **interesting** book, a **moving** story, a **nicely-bound** book, a **beautifully-illustrated** book, a **friendly** man, a **kind** man, a **courteous** man, a **handsome** man.*

214 Nobody, No-one

(i) The pronouns 'nobody' and 'no-one' are singular; they take singular verbs, and other pronouns referring to them must be singular.

*Examples: Nobody **likes** to know that people are criticizing **him**.* (But not 'like to know . . . criticizing them'.)
*No-one likes to be given short change, does **he**?*

(ii) When 'nobody' is used to denote the absence of persons, a plural sense may be attached to it, and a pronoun referring back to it may be plural.

*Example: Nobody has opened this cupboard during my absence, have **they**?*

215 None

(i) When 'none' means 'not one' it takes a singular verb.
*Example: The committee made three suggestions but **none was** acceptable.*

(ii) A singular verb used immediately after a plural noun may sound incorrect, and it is usually possible to reframe the sentence to avoid this.
Example: 'None of the six sprinters was good enough to run in the Olympics' is correct, but 'Of the six sprinters, none was good enough to run in the Olympics' is more easily accepted.

216 No sooner

'No sooner . . .' is followed by 'than', not by 'when'.
*Example: I had **no sooner** sat down **than** the telephone rang.*
(See also **Scarcely** and **Hardly**.)

217 Notable, Notorious

'Notable' means 'worthy of notice'; 'notorious' means 'noted for wrong-doing or undesirable characteristics'.

Examples: *The signing of* Magna Carta *was a **notable** event in British history*
*Some of the most **notorious** prisoners are in the top-security wing.*

218 Not only . . . but also

(i) It is wrong to say, 'He not only called out to me but my wife also'. This is a badly constructed and ambiguous sentence. It should be, 'He called out **not only** to me **but also** to my wife'.
It would be correct to say, 'He **not only** called out to me **but also** waved excitedly'.
(ii) It is no longer regarded as a serious error to omit 'also', provided that the omission does not create the possibility of a misunderstanding. The meaning of the following sentence is still clear if 'also' is omitted. *I **not only** accused him of dishonesty but (**also**) produced evidence to prove it.*

219 Not to worry

This is one of many modern catch-phrases that are quite meaningless. 'Do not worry' or 'I won't worry' would be clearer and more correct.

220 Noun

Nouns are names. They are classified into four groups.
A. (i) **Common nouns** name things or classes of things, *for example, book, road, ship, animal, dog, boy, sister, cousin, doctor, city, river.*
(ii) **Proper nouns** name particular persons, places or things, and are spelt with a capital letter, *for example, Miss Smith, Dr Foster, London, Arabia, River Trent, Uncle Tom's Cabin.*
(iii) **Abstract nouns** name ideas or qualities, *for example, happiness, sorrow, honesty, success, beauty.*
(iv) **Collective nouns** name groups of things, animals or people, *for example, bunch, fleet, flock, swarm, crowd, audience, jury, committee.*
B. Most errors involving the use of nouns are concerned with
(i) the agreement of subject nouns with their verbs;
(ii) the writing of possessive forms; and
(iii) deciding whether certain nouns should be regarded as singular or plural.
For discussion of these difficulties see **Agreement**, **Possessive forms of nouns**, **Singular or plural**, and **Collective nouns**.

75

221 Number of ...

(i) 'A number of people' (meaning 'many people') is plural in sense and so requires a plural verb.

*Example: A number of **people were** injured in the collision.*

(ii) 'The **number** of people' (referring to a figure) is singular and takes a singular verb.

*Example: The **number** of people using public transport **is** decreasing.*

222 Numbers

(i) Many publishers follow the convention of expressing in words numbers up to ten, and this is recommended.

(ii) For larger numbers, figures are more concise and preferable to words.

Example: There are 203 817 voters on the electoral rolls.

However, round figures are conveniently expressed in words, *for example, nearly three thousand voters.*

(iii) An exception to the rule in (i) is made when writing numbers in dates and percentages, and in specific numbers followed by units, *for example, 3rd March 1976,* or *3 March 1976; a discount of 5 per cent; ... purchased 7 yards of carpet; ... ordered 2 pounds of minced steak.*

However, when the reference to numbers and units is casual rather than specific, the numbers are spelt out, *for example, ... about five miles per hour, ... at least ten yards away, ... hesitated for a moment or two, ... I have warned you a hundred times ....*

(iv) In works dealing with technical subjects, in which numbers occur frequently, figures are more convenient and more appropriate than words.

Example: The new engine has a capacity of 4.3 litres and a power output of 153 kilowatts at 4400 revolutions per minute.

(v) Figures should not start a sentence, and should not end a sentence if this can be avoided.

Examples: The fourth of July is an important date in American history. (not '4th July is an important date ... ')
Thirty-seven couples took part in the ballroom dancing competition. (not '37 couples ... ')

(vi) Fractions are written in words with a hyphen.

Example: At least two-thirds of the class have bad colds.

(vii) For decimals figures should always be used, *for example, 2.5, 2.05, 0.25.*

(viii) For clock times, two forms are correct—(*a*) *ten minutes past four, half past nine, six o'clock,* or (*b*) *4.10, 9.30, 6.00* (a.m. or p.m. in each

222 NUMBERS (*continued*)

case). 'A quarter to nine in the morning' is more clumsy than '8.45 a.m.'
Figures and words should not be mixed as in '10 past eight', or 'a quarter
to 3'.

Note: A mixture of figures and words may be used if it is necessary for
clarity, for example, 10 two-hour classes.

(See also **Dates**.)

O

223 Occupier, Occupant

An 'occupier' occupies a house or a business premises on a permanent basis. An 'occupant' occupies, for a short time, a seat in a car, in a theatre, or in a railway carriage.

224 Official, Officious

'Official' refers to the holding of an office or authority.

*Examples: An **official** inquiry will be made into this matter.*

*He is an **official** of the taxation department.*

'Officious' suggests an arrogant manner in carrying out official duties.

*Example: An **officious** gatekeeper tried to prevent us from entering the arena.*

225 One

If a sentence or clause is begun with this impersonal pronoun, it should be completed consistently, using the impersonal or general pronoun rather than a specific one.

Correct: **One** *likes to be remembered for* **one's** *good deeds.*

One *should consider* **oneself** *last.*

Incorrect: **One** *likes to be remembered for* **his** *good deeds.*

One *should consider* **himself** *last.*

'One' should be used sparingly; its repetition soon gives an impression of pomposity.

226 Only

(i) Grammatical correctness requires that the adverb 'only' be placed as near as possible to the word it modifies. 'I spoke **only** to the boy' means that I spoke to nobody else. 'I **only** spoke to the boy' means that I did nothing else but speak. '**Only** I spoke to the boy' means that nobody else spoke to him.

Where this rule is not observed, ambiguity is often the result. However, provided that there is no chance of misunderstanding, sentences which break the rule are not nowadays regarded as 'bad

English'. For example, both of the following sentences are acceptable:
*We need **only** one more goal to win.*
*We **only** need one more goal to win.*
(ii) Observe the differences in meaning which result when the position of 'only' is changed in the following sentences.
***Only** Tom lent me a pound.*
*Tom **only** lent me a pound.*
*Tom lent **only** me a pound.*
*Tom lent me a pound **only**.*
(iii) Is there a better position for 'only' in the following sentences?
(*a*) *He says my uncle only died last week.*
(*b*) *John only came home from hospital on Wednesday.*
(See also **Not only**.)

227 Other

The Murray is longer than any river in Australia. This sentence suggests that the Murray River is not in Australia. It should be '. . . longer than any **other** river in Australia'.

228 Other hand

We are not opposed to your plan; on the other hand we see much merit in it. This is incorrect. The second statement cancels or contradicts the first, and should be introduced by the phrase, 'on the contrary'. The phrase 'on the other hand' should introduce a second statement which contrasts with the first but does not contradict it.
*Example: This heating system is expensive to install; **on the other hand** its operating cost is low.*

229 Otherwise

(i) *We must leave soon, or otherwise we shall be late for our appointment.* 'Or' should be omitted from this sentence, because the alternative expressed by 'or' is already implied in 'otherwise'. It would be correct to say '. . . **or else** we shall be late . . . .'
(ii) 'Otherwise' may be used as an adverb.
*Example: Careless errors spoilt an **otherwise** satisfactory essay.*
(iii) The use of 'otherwise' as (a) a noun, or (b) an adjective is accepted, but not good style. An alternative should be found if possible.

Examples: (*a*) *We must discuss the wisdom or* **otherwise** *of your suggestion.* (We could use another word such as 'foolishness'.)

(*b*) *I am particularly fond of carrots, raw or* **otherwise**. ('. . . raw or cooked.' is an alternative.)

P

230 Participles

A. A participle is a part-verb.

(i) The **present participle** of a verb ends in '-ing', *for example, waiting, dancing, singing*. It is used to form the continuous tense.

*Examples: He is **waiting**.*
*They were **dancing**.*
*She was **singing**.*

(ii) The **past participle** usually ends in '-d', '-ed', '-n', '-en', or '-t', *for example, hoped, walked, known, eaten, slept*. It combines with the verb 'have' to form the perfect tense.

*Examples: I have **eaten**.*
*He has **walked**.*
*We had **hoped**.*
*They have **known**.*
*She has **slept**.*

(iii) When participles combine with auxiliary or 'helper' verbs, for example, 'is', 'am', 'are', 'was', 'were', 'has', 'have', they form complete verbs.

*Examples: I **am waiting**.*
*She **has eaten**.*
*They **have walked**.*

(iv) Confusion of past participle and past tense—see **Verb**.

B. (i) When a sentence is begun with a participle, care is needed in completing the sentence. It is wrong to say, 'Arriving late, the concert had already started'. This suggests that it was the concert that arrived late. We could say, '**Arriving** late, **we** found that the concert had already started'. The person ('we') whose action is implied in the participle ('arriving') must be mentioned in the following main clause.

(ii) When a participle is related to the wrong noun or pronoun in the same sentence we call it an 'unrelated participle'.

Incorrect: (*a*) *Entering the shop, the safe was found blown open.*
(*b*) *After climbing to the summit, the cars below looked tiny.*

>   (c) *Blown down by the gale, our progress was stopped by several large trees.*

Correct: (a) **Entering** *the shop, the* **police** *found . . . .*
          (b) *After* **climbing** *to the summit,* **we** *noticed that . . . .*
          (c) *Our progress was stopped by several large* **trees blown** *down by the wind.*

231 Parts of speech

All words are classified into eight groups called 'parts of speech'. These are: *noun, pronoun, verb, adjective, adverb, preposition, conjunction, interjection.* For definitions, examples, and discussion of correct usage, see separate entries on these parts of speech.

A word is classified according to its function in a particular sentence, and the same word may be used as different parts of speech in different sentences.

Example: The word 'round' is

    a **noun** in: *We won the first* **round**.

    a **verb** in: *I saw the car* **round** *the corner at high speed.*

    an **adjective** in: *A wheel is* **round**.

    an **adverb** in: *The baker comes* **round** *every morning.*

    a **preposition** in: *The teacher came* **round** *the corner unexpectedly.*

232 Passed, Past

(i) When the word is a verb the correct form is 'passed'.

Examples: *We* **passed** *a number of cars.*
           Jane **passed** *her examinations.*

(ii) For parts of speech other than the verb, 'past' is correct.

Examples: *The procession has gone* **past**.
           Who went **past** *the window just now?*

233 Per

This Latin word, meaning 'by' or 'for each', is used in business English in phrases such as '**per** *annum*' (for each year), '**per** week', '**per** day', '**per** dozen'. In normal English it is better to avoid mixtures of Latin and English as seen in '**per** year', '**per** head'. English alone is quite effective, *for example, fifty pounds a week.*

234 Perfect tense

A. Perfect tense is a form of the verb that indicates a perfected or completed action. The perfect tense has three main forms, each of which uses part of the verb 'to have' (have, has, had).

(i) *I **have finished** my essay.* **Present perfect** tense, referring to an action that is completed now.

(ii) *I **had finished** my essay before morning break.* **Past perfect** tense referring to an action that was completed at some time in the past.

(iii) *By four o'clock I **shall have finished** my essay.* **Future perfect** tense, referring to an action that will be completed at some time in the future.

B. Care is needed to avoid the common error of using a double perfect.

Incorrect: (a) *I wish I **had have** known earlier that you were coming.*

(b) *I should **have liked** to **have met** your cousin.*

Correct: (a) *I wish I **had known** earlier . . . .*

(b) *I should **have liked** to meet your cousin.*

*I should like to **have met** your cousin.*

(See also **Tense**.)

235 Personal(ly)

'Personal' and 'personally' are often used unnecessarily, as in, 'A **personal** friend told me' and 'I **personally** felt slighted . . . .' All friends are personal, and in the second example 'personally' merely repeats 'I' in sense.

'Personal' and 'personally' are correctly used when it is necessary to distinguish between, for example, a private and an official viewpoint.

*Examples: The Prime Minister made it clear that he was expressing a **personal** opinion.*

***Personally** I advise you not to pay this fee, although as an official I have to demand payment.*

236 Personal, Personnel

'Personal' means 'belonging to a person', *for example, **personal** property, a **personal** service, **personal** appearance.*

'Personnel' refers to the persons engaged in an industrial or business concern or in a service, *for example, all the army **personnel** in a district, a **personnel** officer to select new staff members.*

237 Phrase

A. (i) A phrase is a group of words which has the function of a noun, an adjective, or an adverb in a sentence. It has no subject and verb, but may contain a part-verb such as

a present participle: *eating a pie;*

a past participle: *broken by the wind;*

an infinitive: *to bake some buns.*

Many phrases begin with a preposition, *for example*, **in** *the car*, **after** *the party*, **with** *her sister*.

(ii) The following examples show the functions of some of the most common types of phrases.

Examples: That girl **with fair hair** *is Norwegian.* (adjective phrase, describing the girl)

Many flowers bloom **in spring***.* (adverb phrase of time)

The accident happened **at this intersection***.* (adverb phrase of place)

The motorist drove **with great care***.* (adverb phrase of manner)

We have to learn **how to live with others***.* (noun phrase, telling or naming what we have to learn)

B. Care must be taken to place phrases correctly. The sentences following show what happens when phrases are placed incorrectly.

Farmer Brown found a nest of field mice **harvesting his wheat***.*

I have inherited an antique chair from my aunt **with beautifully carved legs***.*

238 Plurals

A. There is a good deal of uncertainty about the spelling of the plural forms of some nouns. As with spelling in general, the best advice one can give is 'Consult a dictionary'. Begin to cultivate this habit now by consulting a dictionary to find the plurals of these words: *cactus, crisis, octopus, datum, formula, index, oasis, fungus.*

B. The following points should be noted.

(i) Words ending in 'y' form the plural by changing 'y' to 'i' and adding 'es', provided that the 'y' is preceded by a consonant, *for example, baby, babies; army, armies; pony, ponies; duty, duties; story, stories.*

But if a vowel precedes the 'y', simply add 's', *for example, keys, valleys, monkeys, donkeys.*

(ii) Most words ending in 'o' add 'es' to form the plural, *for example, potatoes, tomatoes, negroes.* Common exceptions are: *pianos, contraltos, photos, studios, folios, solos.*

(iii) In compounded words, the plural is formed from the most important element, the noun. However, usage varies, especially when both elements are nouns. *For example, son(s)-in-law, court(s) martial, commander(s)-in-chief, governor(s) general* (here 'general' is an adjective), *lieutenant-general(s)* (here 'general' is a noun), *hanger(s)-on, go-between(s), maid-servant(s), men-servants.*

(iv) When titles are reduced to initials, 's' is added to the abbreviated form, *for example, Justices of the Peace, J.P.s; Bachelors of Arts, B.A.s; Members of Parliament, M.P.s.*

239 Plus

This is one of the over-worked words. Its use should be confined to (a) mathematical statements, and (b) statements about two things which make a well-recognized combination.

*Example: The price is ten pounds **plus** VAT.*

'Plus' should **not** be used as a synonym of 'and', 'in addition to', or 'together with'. The following two sentences are **incorrect**.

Examples: The taxi driver drove his two passengers plus luggage to the airport.

The staff comprises a manager plus two assistants.

240 Possessive forms of nouns

The possessive forms of nouns are written according to the following rules:

(i) **Singular nouns** are made possessive by adding ' 's ', *for example, a lady's purse; a fox's tail; a boy's knife; Tom's father; Mr Smith's car.* If the addition of ' 's ', results in an unpleasant hissing sound, the apostrophe alone may be used. *For example, Moses' leadership; for goodness' sake.*

(ii) When several nouns are used together, the ' 's ' is used with the last one only, *for example, my sister-in-law's home; Mr Jones the Chairman's report; Germany, France and Italy's co-operation; Moran and Cato's shop.*

When the nouns are clearly separated, the 's is used with each, *for example, Mozart's and Beethoven's symphonies.*

(iii) The **possessive plural** of nouns is formed by

(a) adding the apostrophe only to plural nouns ending in 's', *for example, the boys' hats; the ladies' purses; the foxes' tails; the wolves' dens.*

(b) adding the apostrophe **and** 's' to plural nouns which do not end in 's', *for example, the men's cars; the women's faces, the children's fathers; the geese's eggs; the mice's tails.*

(iv) Note that the apostrophe is not used in the possessives 'its' and 'yours', *for example, on its nest; my pen and yours.*

241 Possessive pronouns and adjectives

A. (i) *This coat is **mine**.*

*These books are **yours**.*

*That pen is **his**.*

In these sentences, 'mine', 'yours', and 'his' are possessive pronouns, related to nouns which have been mentioned, that is, 'coat', 'books', and 'pen' respectively.

(ii) *This is **my** coat.*
*These are **your** books.*
*That is **his** pen.*

In these sentences, 'my', 'your', and 'his' are adjectives qualifying the nouns 'coat', 'books', and 'pen' respectively.

B. (i) *The thief has taken mine and your coat.* This is incorrect; 'mine' is a pronoun and has no clear meaning until the noun for which it stands has been mentioned, as in, 'The thief has taken your coat and mine'.

(ii) *His and her cars were damaged in the collision.*
The collectors have been to your and my homes.

These sentences are grammatically correct, but are awkward. It sounds better to say 'his car and hers', and 'your home and mine'.

242 Practical, Practicable

A **practical** idea is one that is known to be successful or effective in the given circumstances.

A **practicable** plan is one that appears to be capable of being put into practice.

*Examples: This plan has never been used, but I believe it is **practicable**.*
*We are interested in **practical** rather than experimental designs.*

243 Practice, Practise. See **Advice**

244 Precede, Proceed

'Precede' means 'go before'.

*Example: In the procession the Mayor will **precede** all the other citizens.*

'Proceed' means 'to go forward'.

*Example: You should **proceed** carefully in this matter.*
*The funeral **proceeded** slowly up the hill.*

245 Prefer, Preferable

Both these words are followed by the preposition 'to'.

*Examples: Many people **prefer** sandwiches **to** cakes.*
*Playing sport is **preferable to** merely watching it.*

It is wrong to use the expressions 'prefer more than' and 'more preferable'.

246 Preposition

A. (i) A preposition is a word used with a noun or pronoun to show its relation to some other word in the sentence. For example, a car could be **in** a garage, **near** a garage, or **outside** a garage. A box could be **on, near,** or **under** a table. The words showing the relationships— 'in', 'near', 'outside', 'on', 'under'—are prepositions.

(ii) Until recently it was considered wrong to end a sentence with a preposition. Today we judge such sentences by their general effect, and many are accepted because they seem natural.

*Examples: I gave the child a spoon to eat **with**.*
*Where do you come **from**?*
*What are you complaining **about**?*
*Nobody likes to be laughed **at**.*

(iii) The English language includes a great number of **prepositional phrases**, that is, certain words followed by particular prepositions.
Examples:

*afflicted **with** bronchitis*	*sensitive **to** the cold*
*essential **to** life*	*alien **to** his nature*
*confide **in** a friend*	*conversant **with** a subject*
*relevant **to** a subject*	*congratulate **on** winning*
*susceptible **to** (colds, flattery)*	*responsible **to** a person*
*exempt **from** taxation*	*responsible **for** damage* (or a thing entrusted)

*Other examples are: conform **to**; comply **with**; compatible **with**; averse **to**; prevail **upon**; deficient **in**; identical **with**; oblivious **of**; compare **to*** (to show similarities); *compare **with*** (to note points of difference).

B. **Common errors in the use of prepositions:**

(i) *Ann sits with Joan and I.* After a preposition (with) the object form of the pronoun is used. Say, 'with Joan and **me**'.

(ii) *I disagree and disapprove of your handling of this problem.* Two different prepositions are required here. Say, 'I disagree **with** and disapprove **of** . . . .'

(iii) *The problem to which your recent letter refers to has now been solved.* The preposition is often wrongly repeated; in this sentence the second 'to' is unnecessary.

(iv) *Temperatures in Africa are generally higher than Europe.* The error here is in the omission of a preposition; 'higher than **in** Europe' is correct. (See also, **Between; Among, Between;** and **Besides, Beside.**)

247 Principal, Principle

In all contexts 'principal' means 'chief' or 'first in importance', *for*

example, the **principal** *of a college; the* **principal** *causes or results of an event; my* **principal** *objection to a suggestion; the* **principal** *performers in a stage show; the* **principal** *deposit which earns interest in a bank.*
'Principle' refers to a law governing natural events or human behaviour, *for example, Newton's* **principles** *of gravity; a man of high* **principles***; a mean* **unprincipled** *action; object to a law on* **principle***.*

248 Prior

'Prior' is an adjective meaning 'previous', and is correctly used before a noun, as in 'a prior engagement'. It should not be used as a preposition, as it is in the sentence, 'We visited a friend prior to going to the theatre'. Say, '. . . before going to . . . .'

249 Pronoun

A. (i) A pronoun is a word used instead of a noun. The use of pronouns allows us to refer to people or things without actually naming them, and this helps us to avoid awkward repetition. For example, the sentence, 'Jean told Tom that **she** would help **him**' would in the absence of pronouns have to be written, 'Jean told Tom that Jean would help Tom'.
(ii) There are about eight different types of pronouns, but they all have in common the function of being used instead of a noun.
Frequently used pronouns are: *I, me, mine, we, us, ours, he, him, his, she, her, hers, it, they, them, theirs, who, whose, which, that, myself, himself, herself, itself, themselves, somebody, anybody, everybody, nobody, anything.*
(iii) A word that is a pronoun (taking the place of a noun) in one sentence may be an adjective (qualifying a noun) in another context. Words are classified according to their functions.
Examples: Pronoun use: ***This*** *is mine.*
  These *are not ripe.*
  If you have lost your knife, borrow ***his***.
Adjective use: ***This*** *pen is mine.*
  These *plums are not ripe.*
  Borrow ***his*** *knife.*
B. **Pronouns must be used with care.** Often when they are used carelessly the meaning of the sentence becomes uncertain.
Examples:
(*a*) *When the policeman came face to face with the hijacker he shot him.*
  (Who did the shooting—the policeman or the hijacker?)
(*b*) *Jack told his brother that he had behaved badly.* (Who behaved badly? Was Jack making a confession, or criticizing his brother?)

(*c*) *Your dog seems to like me better than you.* (Does the dog prefer me? Or does the dog like me more than you do?)

Usually it is not difficult to avoid this type of ambiguity. For example, sentence (*b*) could be written, 'Jack confessed to his brother . . .' or 'Jack accused his brother . . . .'

C. (i) Singular pronouns are used to refer to singular nouns; plural pronouns refer to plural nouns. The following sentence breaks this rule.

A small car is economical to run: they are becoming increasingly popular for that reason.

A plural pronoun 'they' refers to a singular noun, 'car'; either the noun or the pronoun must be changed so that both are either singular or plural.

(ii) Emphatic pronouns (*myself, yourself, himself,* etc.) are for emphasis and should not be used as subjects.

*Incorrect: My brother and **myself** both like jazz.*

*Correct: My brother and **I** both like jazz.*

*I blamed him, but I broke it **myself.***

(iii) It is sometimes necessary to supply an understood verb in order to determine the form of the pronoun to be used.

*Incorrect: John is older than **me.***

*Correct: John is older than **I** (am).*

D. (i) The pronouns 'anybody', 'nobody', 'everybody', 'each', 'either', and 'neither' used as subjects take a singular verb and a singular pronoun following.

*Examples: If **each does his** best, we shall win.*

***Everybody was** present for the rehearsal.*

*The boys are ready; **each has** brought **his** own lunch.*

*Two girls have applied; **either is** suitable for the position.*

*Two motorists drove past, but **neither was** willing to help us.*

(See also **Anyone, Everyone**, and **Nobody**.)

(ii) When pronouns of different persons are used, they are placed in the order:

(a) Third person—the person(s) spoken **about** (*he, she, they*)

(b) Second person—the person(s) spoken **to** (*you*)

(c) First person—the person(s) speaking (*I, we*)

*Example: **He, you** and **I** will travel in the same car.*

(See also **Case**.)

250 Proximity

The rule of proximity says that a word or group of words should be placed near the word to which it refers. When this rule is broken the result is often confusion or absurdity.

*Examples: For sale: piano by a widow with four children **recently tuned***
    *A vast plain was seen by the explorers **stretching away to the west***
    ***Flying towards the marshes** we saw a number of wild geese.*

It is a simple matter to correct these sentences by placing the **bold** phrases next to the nouns to which they refer.

(See also **Only**, and **Such**.)

251 Punctuation

When we speak, we stop at the end of a sentence. We also make pauses, thus helping the listener to follow our meaning. By changing the pitch of the voice we can indicate a question or an exclamation. In writing, we indicate these pauses and changes of expression by means of a system of punctuation marks. It is important to use only as many stops as are essential to convey meaning clearly. Over-punctuation is confusing and irritating.

(See **Full stop, Comma, Semicolon, Colon, Dash, Hyphen, Question mark, Exclamation mark, Apostrophe, Direct speech,** and **Quotation marks**.)

252 Purposely, Purposefully

'Purposely' means 'intentionally'; 'purposefully' means 'in a determined manner'.

*Examples: I am sure he did not bump you **purposely**.*
    *We must attack this problem **purposefully** if we wish to achieve anything.*

Q

253 Query

This word does not mean 'ask' or 'inquire'; it is wrongly used in the sentence, 'I shall query the shipping agent about departure dates'. It is correctly used in the sense of inquiry or question, with doubt or suspicion in mind.

*Examples: The chairman **queried** the accuracy of the minutes of the previous meeting.*

*The accountant **queried** the correctness of the balance sheet.*

254 Question

The next item on the agenda is the election of a delegate to attend the international conference. I am sure all members will be interested to discuss this question. The item is not introduced as a question; therefore 'subject' or 'matter' should be used instead of 'question'. 'Question' is correctly used in, 'You ask whether we are sending a delegate to the conference. We shall discuss that **question** now'.

255 Question mark

This is used at the end of a direct question or after a statement which is really a question.

Examples: Has the postman been yet?

You really expect me to believe that?

In sentences that include quotations, question marks (and exclamation marks) are placed within the inverted commas if they belong to the quotations as in Example (*a*) following; otherwise they are placed outside the inverted commas as in Example (*b*).

Examples: (a) My father said, "Why are you looking so worried?"

The constable said, "May I see your driving licence?"

(b) Why did he say, "You are wise to reject the offer"?

Why did the constable say, "Your brakes are not very effective"?

(See also **Quotation marks.**)

256 Quite

Be careful of this word. Telling a person that his playing, singing or acting was 'quite good' seems to damn him with faint praise. At best it shows a lack of enthusiasm. The use of 'quite' rarely adds anything to the meaning of a sentence.

Example: He won (quite) a large sum in the lottery.

257 Quiz

This word is used as a verb and as a noun, particularly in reference to radio and television programs involving tests of knowledge. It is sometimes used colloquially to refer to an oral examination. It should not be used seriously to refer to a formal examination or to a questionnaire.

258 Quotation marks

(i) Quotation marks or inverted commas are used to mark off spoken or quoted words from the rest of the text.

The modern practice is to use double quotes (" ") as normal, and single quotes (' ') for less common quotations such as those occurring within a passage that is itself quoted.

Examples: (a) *The coach said, "We can win this game if we play with determination."*

    (b) *The question was "Name the author of the line 'A little learning is a dangerous thing' and the poem in which it appears."*

    She said, "What do you mean by 'perhaps'?"

(ii) Publishing houses do not agree on the punctuation of sentences which include quotations, but normal practice is to use the stop before closing the quotation marks.

Example: John called out, "There is a fish on your line."

(iii) If the quoted passage consists of more than one paragraph, a single quote (') at the beginning of the first paragraph and at the end of the final paragraph (') is sufficient.

(iv) Commas must be used to mark off direct speech from the rest of the sentence.

Examples: (a) *He whispered, "Please pass this note to Tom."*

    (b) *"We have run out of petrol," said Frank.*

    (c) *"I have a feeling," said the detective, "that you are telling lies to protect somebody."*

    (d) *"Here are the plans," he said. "They will cost you a thousand pounds."*

After a break as in (c), the quotation continues without a capital letter, as the words spoken form one sentence. However, after a break as in (d), a capital letter is required, as the words spoken form two sentences.

(v) If a quoted passage ends with a question or an exclamation, a question mark or an exclamation mark is used.
Examples: "Have we run out of petrol?" asked Jane.
   "Oh, don't say we have run out of petrol!" exclaimed Sue.
(vi) Question marks and exclamation marks are placed within the inverted commas if they belong to the quotation, as in (v) above, and Example (*a*) following; otherwise they are placed outside the inverted commas as in Example (*b*).
Examples: (*a*) *My aunt said, "Why are you looking so puzzled?"*
      "Oh, you stupid boy!" exclaimed the teacher.
   (*b*) *Why did she say, "That is a very selfish attitude"?*
Sometimes a quoted question or exclamation is contained within a sentence that is also a question or exclamation, and two symbols are required.
Examples: Did he really say, "Where do you keep your jewels?"?
   How frightening was their cry, "We conquer or die!"!
However, the modern tendency is to avoid two full stops, and to use the first only.
Example: His only comment was, "I am not interested."
(vii) Single quotes may be used as an alternative to italic type, to denote names of ships, trains, etc.
Examples: We crossed the Atlantic on the 'Queen Elizabeth'.
   'The Flying Scotsman' is a famous train.
(viii) Titles of articles or chapters in a publication are usually placed within single quotes. The name of the publication itself may be in single quotes, in italics, or underlined.
Examples: I have been reading 'War and Peace'.
      The lecturer asked us to read the essay entitled 'Social Cohesion and Human Nature', in Bertrand Russell's *Authority and the Individual.*
(See also **Titles**.)
(ix) Single quotes are placed round a word or phrase to draw attention to it. This may be done when the word or expression is of special significance, or is used in a special sense, or is slang or a newly-coined term, or is meant to express sarcasm.
Examples: My grandfather described my companions as 'a bad lot'.
   'Interesting', you say. I think 'eccentric' would describe him more accurately.
   The new girl said, "My name is Christina, but I am called 'Tina' by all my friends."

93

"The 'soup', as you call it, tastes like washing up water," I complained.

(See also **Direct, Indirect Speech**.)

R

259 Raise, Rise, Arise

'Raise' is a transitive verb; its action goes over to some object. *For example, men raise their hats, shopkeepers raise prices, school fetes are held to raise money, cranes are used to raise heavy objects, an employer may raise a man's wages.*

The past tense is 'raised'.

Example: He raised his hat.

The past participle is also 'raised'.

Example: The landlord has raised the rent.

'Rise' is intransitive; there is no object affected by the action. *For example, the sun rises, people rise (from their seats), prices rise.*

The past tense is 'rose'.

Example: He rose and went out.

The past participle is 'risen'.

Examples: The moon has risen.
Prices have risen sharply.

'Arise' means 'to come about'. *For example, storms arise, doubts arise, a quarrel arose, an embarrassing situation has arisen.*

260 Re

(i) 'Re' is not an accepted abbreviation of 'regarding' or 'referring to'; used as such it is an example of commercial jargon.

Example: Enclosed are details re our economy class fares.

(ii) 'Re' is a shortened form of the Latin phrase '*in re*' meaning 'in the matter of'. It is widely and legitimately used in legal documents, and is acceptable in formal headings of official or business letters.

Examples: re (or in re) John Richards, deceased;
re the Marshall Bequest.

(iii) 'Re' should **not** be used in normal prose.

Examples: Re your enquiry of 5th July I wish to advise you that....
I wish to make a complaint re the plumbing in the house I purchased from you.
I was interested to hear the Chancellor's comments re the new taxation policy.

In sentences such as these, 'about', 'regarding', 'concerning', 'referring to', or 'with reference to' can be used.

261 Real, Really

'Real' and 'really', like 'actually' and 'definitely', often add nothing to the sense of a statement, and are therefore better omitted.

Examples: He said that the existence of nuclear weapons is a (real) threat to peace.
News of Tom's success comes as a (real) surprise.
That is a (really) lovely painting.

262 Reason ... because ... See Because

263 Recover, Re-cover

*Examples: A worn umbrella could be **re-covered** and so made fit for use again.*
*A person who lost his umbrella might be lucky enough to **recover** it from the finder.*
*Most patients **recover** after an operation for appendicitis.*

(See also **Hyphen**.)

264 Redundancy

Redundancy of expression—that is, the use of unnecessary words—is a fault to be avoided. In these examples of redundancy, the superfluous words are in **bold type**.

*Examples: I like this coat **equally** as well as the other.*
*The **future** prospects of the wool industry are brighter now.*
*Salmon abound **in great numbers** in the streams of Canada.*
*It is unwise to have **false** illusions about one's ability.*
*The result of this strike is **that it has brought about** the closing of many factories.*
*The children were **all** unanimous in voting for a holiday.*
*The examiner allowed me to refer **back** to my notes.*

Most of these examples of redundancy are also examples of tautology, that is, the repetition of the same idea in different words.

(See also **Tautology**.)

265 Refute. See Deny

266 Regretful, Regrettable

'Regretful' means 'full of regret'; a 'regrettable' action is one that causes regret.

*Example: That was a **regrettable** mistake; I feel very **regretful** about its consequences.*

267 Relative pronoun

(i) A relative pronoun combines the functions of a pronoun (used instead of a noun) and a conjunction (combining two clauses). The most common relative pronouns are 'who', 'whom', 'whose', 'which', and 'that'.

*Example: That is the man **who** asked me to direct him.*

'Who' is the equivalent of 'man'. It joins the two thoughts: (a) A man asked me to direct him; and (b) That is the man.

(ii) A relative pronoun and the clause it introduces should be placed as near as possible to its antecedent (that is, the noun or pronoun to which it refers). This rule is broken in the following sentences with humorous results.

*Examples: The **car** was left outside the home of the scoutmaster **which** had over-heated.*

*We are sending your **watch** by special messenger **which** we have cleaned and regulated.*

The remedy is to place the clauses introduced by the relative pronoun 'which' next after the antecedents 'car' and 'watch'.

(iii) If the relative pronoun 'which' is used to refer to a whole clause, care should be taken to clarify meaning, usually by the use of a comma.

Incorrect: A visiting hunter shot the man-eating tiger which delighted the villagers. (Was it the man-eating tiger that delighted the villagers?)

Correct: A visiting hunter shot the man-eating tiger, which delighted the villagers.

The villagers were delighted when a visiting hunter shot the man-eating tiger.

(See also **Which**.)

(iv) *He is a boy **whom** I am sure can be trusted.* In this sentence the use of 'whom' is an error. The inclusion of 'I am sure' helps to hide the fact that the word required is the **subject** of the verb 'can be trusted'. The subject form is 'who', that is, 'He is a boy **who**, I am sure, can be trusted'.

*Example: There is the man **who**, I am sure, stole the watch.*

268 Replica

A replica is not merely a copy; it is a copy of an object by the craftsman who made the original. A present-day artist cannot produce a replica of a work by an eighteenth-century artist.

269 Respective(ly)

(i) This word is used to express a one-to-one correspondence between single items in two groups or series.

*Examples: John and Henry play football and hockey **respectively**.* (This means that John plays football and Henry plays hockey.)

*The three managers reported on the level of business in their **respective** departments.* (The managers of, say, the clothing, hardware and sporting departments of a large store each gave a report on his own department.)

(ii) There are several common errors in the use of 'respective' and 'respectively'.

*Examples: The heats were won by Smith, Thompson and Williams **respectively**.* (To justify the use of 'respectively' we should say, 'The first three heats . . .' or specify the heats in some other way.)

*We are all entitled to our **respective** opinions.* ('Respective' does not mean the same as 'own', which is required here.)

*Volvo, Mercedes, Fiat and Alfa Romeo cars are made in Sweden, Germany and Italy **respectively**.* (This is confusing because four items, the cars, cannot have a one-to-one correspondence with three items, the countries.)

Sentences built around 'respective' and 'respectively' are confusing to many people. It is advisable, and usually not difficult, to avoid their use.

270 Reverent, Reverend

One has a 'reverent' feeling or attitude towards things regarded as sacred.

'Reverend' is a title given to a clergyman, *for example, the **Rev.** R. J. Thomas, the **Rev.** Raymond Thomas, the **Rev.** Mr Thomas.* ('Rev.' is **not** used with the surname alone as in 'the Rev. Thomas'.)

A clergyman is introduced as 'the Reverend . . .', but is addressed as 'Mister . . .'.

271 Review, Revue

'Review' is used as a verb and as a noun.

*Examples: The commander **reviewed** (inspected) the troops.* (verb)

*Ted had to write a book **review** for his English teacher.* (noun)

A 'revue' is a variety show, usually musical and bright, with a theme or slight story connecting the items.

S

272 Same

We thank you for your suggestions and will give same our early attention.

We are planning to purchase new machinery and install same before the end of the financial year.

These sentences show the use of 'same' as a substitute for a pronoun such as 'it' or 'them'. This is an example of business jargon that should be avoided.

273 Scarcely

'Scarcely', 'hardly' and 'barely' are followed by 'when'.

*Examples: We had **scarcely** reached the hut **when** the rain came down in torrents.*

*The diver had **barely** reached the rock **when** a huge shark appeared.*

Note that a similar sentence can be built around the words 'No sooner . . . than . . .'.

*Example: **No sooner** had the diver reached the rock **than** a huge shark appeared.*

(See also **Hardly** and **No sooner**.)

274 Sceptic, Septic, Cynic

'Sceptic' is often confused with two other words—with one because of similarity of sound, with the other because of an association of meaning.

A **sceptic** (pronounced *skeptik*) is a person who is reluctant to believe.

'**Septic**' is an adjective meaning 'liable to cause blood-poisoning'.

A **cynic** shows contempt for human nature and suspicion of mankind's ideals.

275 Semicolon

The semicolon (;) marks a longer pause than that indicated by a comma. It is used to separate units of a sentence that are grammatically independent but related in meaning.

Examples: We are not going to be put off with excuses; we demand
strong and immediate action.
To err is human; to forgive, divine.

276 Sentences—Qualities

A sentence is a group of words that makes sense. Every sentence has
a verb (expressing an action) and a subject (naming the doer of the
action). Sometimes the subject or the verb is not expressed but
understood.

Examples: 'Who broke the cup?' 'Tom (did).'
'(You) Come here.'

(i) **Sentences should be complete and clear.** A competent writer can
set down a sequence of incomplete but effective sentences, *for
example, Twilight. Red in the west. A glow on the wood.* But the
incomplete sentences produced by the average writer are uninten-
tional, and confusing if not meaningless.

Equally confusing is the sentence which begins with a certain
construction, and then switches to a different construction.

Examples: Having eaten a hearty meal and being tired from the
day's work, and so I did not go for my usual evening swim.
The spectators, though they expected to see a thrilling
match, but they were disappointed.

Written expression should always be re-read to make sure that each
sentence is complete and clear.

(ii) **Sentences should have variety.** It is possible to use a variety of
sentence patterns to express an idea or a combination of ideas. For
example, if we take the ideas expressed in the sentences 'Tom fell
heavily.' and 'Tom was not hurt.' we may combine these ideas using
at least three different constructions.

Examples: (a) Falling heavily, Tom was not hurt.
(b) When he fell heavily, Tom was not hurt.
(c) Tom fell heavily, but was not hurt.

To avoid monotony it is important to give **variety** to sentences—
variety in **construction**, variety in **length**, variety in sentence **begin-
nings.** But it is also important to consider the relative effectiveness of
the alternative constructions. In the example given, sentence (c) is the
most effective in bringing out the unexpected outcome of Tom's
heavy fall.

To sum up—effective writing requires sentences that are complete,
clear, and varied in length and construction.

Two exercises:

(a) How many variations of this line of poetry can you write, using

the same words but in different order? *The plowman homeward plods his weary way.*
(b) Ask a friend to write a sentence about a subject you suggest. Then express the same idea in other sentences using different sentence patterns. Is any one sentence clearly superior or inferior to the others?

277 Sentences—Types

A. **Simple sentence.** The simplest type of sentence is appropriately called a 'simple' sentence. It consists of two parts, the **subject** and the **predicate**. The subject names something; the predicate is what is said about the subject. The shortest sentence consists of two words— a noun as subject and a verb as the predicate, *for example, Dogs bark. Cats purr. Children play.*

We can enlarge the subject and the predicate by adding adjectives, adverbs, and phrases. For example, 'Children play' can be expanded to, 'Most of the **children** from the nearby houses **play** in this park on fine days'. This is still a simple sentence; it has only one subject (children), and one verb (play) which is the keyword of the predicate. The predicate of a sentence may include, in addition to the verb, one or more parts: an **object**, a **complement**, an **adverbial part**. When the action of a verb takes effect on a person or thing, that person or thing is the **object** of the verb, for example, the words 'strangers', 'cakes' and 'sweets' in these two sentences.

*Dogs bite **strangers**.*
*Most children eat **cakes and sweets**.*

Some verbs which express a state rather than an action, do not complete a statement about the subject, *for example, A horse is ...*, or *Tommy was ...* ; something has to be added to complete the sense. The words added are called the 'complement' (the completing part) of the verb, for example, 'ill', 'a quadruped', and 'a naughty child' in these sentences.

*Jane became **ill**.*
*A horse is a **quadruped**.*
*Tommy was **a naughty child**.*

Words and phrases which tell how, why, when, and where the action (expressed by the verb) is done, form the **adverb part** of the sentence. This is sometimes called the 'extension' or the 'adverbial adjunct'.

The table shows some common patterns of simple sentences. The nouns and pronouns which are the true subjects and objects are in *bold* type.

101

Subject	Predicate			
	verb	object	complement	abverbial parts
Mr Smith	*painted*	*his **house***		*last-weekend.*
Canberra	*is*		*the capital of Australia.*	
*This **lane***	*is*		*beautiful*	*in autumn.*
*The **accident***	*happened*			*at that crossing.*
Who	*damaged*	*this **chair**?*		
*****(You)**	*Come*			*here, at once.*
The boys	*elected*	**me**	*captain.*	
Jones, *our opening batsman*	*swept*	*the **ball***		*to the boundary.*

* This subject is 'understood'—that is, not necessarily expressed

(See also **Case**.)

B. Complex and compound sentences. Simple sentences (clauses) are linked together by conjunctions to form complex and compound sentences.

A **simple** sentence has one principal or main clause.

A **complex** sentence has one main clause, and one or more dependent or subordinate clauses which perform the functions of nouns, adjectives and adverbs, and are classified accordingly.

A **compound** sentence has two or more principal clauses of equal grammatical importance. It may have one or more subordinate clauses in addition to the principal clauses.

If we combine the two clauses or simple sentences 'Tom fell over.' and 'Tom broke his arm.' we can form either

(i) a compound sentence consisting of two principal clauses of equal importance—'**Tom fell over** and **broke his arm**.'; or

(ii) a complex sentence, consisting of a principal clause and a subordinate clause (an adverb clause of time)—'**Tom broke his arm** when he fell over'. If we write 'When Tom fell over, **he broke his arm**', we have the same types of clauses in reversed order, that is, an adverb clause followed by the principal clause.

C. It is an interesting and useful exercise to combine sentences in different ways then consider whether one of the new sentences conveys the intended meaning more successfully than the others.

Example (i): ***Tom tried to rescue his dog from the well. Tom fell in.***

(*a*) *While trying to rescue his dog from the well, Tom fell in.* (simple sentence)

(*b*) *When Tom tried to rescue his dog from the well, he fell in.* (complex sentence; adverb clause and principal clause)

(*c*) *Tom tried to rescue his dog from the well, but he fell in.* (compound sentence; principal clause and principal clause)

Do you agree that sentence (*c*) is less satisfactory than the other two?

Example (ii): ***A wild buffalo charged at the hunter. The hunter took refuge in a tree.***

(*a*) *A wild buffalo charged at the hunter and he took refuge in a tree.*

(*b*) *When a wild buffalo charged at him, the hunter took refuge in a tree.*

(*c*) *A wild buffalo charged at the hunter who took refuge in a tree.*

Which of these three sentences do you consider to be most satisfactory?

D. **Sentences to combine for practice:**

(a) The thief crept up to the window. He peered into the room.

(b) The hikers travelled about twenty miles. They made their camp beside a pleasant stream.

(c) The rabbits saw us approaching. They scampered into their burrows.

(d) The fisherman warned the boys of their danger. The boys proceeded no further up the cliff.

278 Shades of meaning

A student increases his ability to use language effectively by extending his vocabulary. This involves not only adding progressively to his store of word meanings, but also learning to distinguish between words that have similar basic meanings. How, for example, would we define a 'foreigner', and under what circumstances would we call him an 'alien', an 'exile', a 'refugee', or an 'immigrant'? What is an emblem, and is it the same as a symbol? Is a signal also a symptom? Is there any difference between a facsimile and a replica? Is a myth the same as a legend?

List (*a*) below consists of a number of words, all of which convey the general idea of elimination. Can you match these verbs with the items in List (*b*)?

103

List (a) abolish, exterminate, eradicate, extinguish, demolish, obliterate, delete, annihilate
List (b) a fire, a nest of ants, a tax, an offensive comment, an army, weeds, a building, an inscription on a monument

A student who wishes to expand his vocabulary will derive much assistance from three basic reference books: a dictionary, a dictionary of synonyms and antonyms, and Roget's *Thesaurus of Words and Phrases.* (See also **Use of dictionary** and **Synonyms.**)

279 Shall, Will

(i) In the simple future tense, 'shall' is used after the pronouns 'I' and 'we'; 'will' is used after other nouns and pronouns.
Examples: ***I shall*** *wait until he comes.*
               They will *be pleased to see you.*
               John will *be at the party.*

(ii) When determination is implied, the normal usage explained in (i) is reversed.
Examples: ***I (We) will*** *vote for him, whether you approve or not.*
               You shall *pay for this insult, I assure you.*

However, there is a tendency, even among writers of note, to ignore this rule and to express determination through the whole sentence rather than depend on the effect created by the use of 'shall' or 'will'.

(iii) To express mere willingness, 'will' may be used in all cases.
Example: ***I will*** *find a taxi for you, and* ***Charles will*** *bring your luggage.*

280 Should, Would

The traditional rules governing the use of 'should' and 'would' are the same as those relating to 'shall' and 'will' (q.v.). But here too the distinctions are breaking down. To complicate matters, 'should' and 'would' each have several different meanings. For example, 'should' is a **future** form of 'shall' in 'He asked whether I **should** be home by four o'clock'; but it also expresses **supposition** in 'If he **should** fail to appear . . .', and moral **obligation** in 'I **should** visit my sick aunt'.

When such complications exist, distinctions between pairs of words like 'would' and 'should' tend to break down. The following examples provide a useful guide to modern usage.
Examples: (a) *I* ***should*** *like to see the Niagara Falls.*
             I said I ***should*** *have the job finished by the week-end.*
      (b) *He* ***would*** *go; nobody could persuade him to wait.*
             I have no regrets; I ***would*** *do the same thing again.*
             ('Would' used to express determination.)

(c) *If I should fail, my parents would be disappointed.*
    If he should complain, ignore him.
('Should' used to express supposition or condition.)
'Shall' or 'will' in a main clause should not be followed by 'should' or
'would' in a subordinate clause.
Incorrect: I shall be grateful if you would reply promptly.
Correct: I shall be . . . if you will . . . . ;
        I should be . . . if you would . . . .

281 Simile
A simile is a figure of speech in which two different things are
compared because they are alike in some respect. The comparison is
introduced through the words 'as' or 'like'.
*Examples: Tom can swim **like** a fish.*
        *The fog hung over the city **like** a grey blanket.*
        *That weight-lifter is **as** strong as a bull.*
Many similes are used so often that they now offer little stimulation to a
reader's thought or imagination, *for example, as geen as grass, as heavy
as lead.* A writer needs to seek appropriate new images. For example, 'his
hair is as black as night' is less effective than 'his hair looks as if he wore
boot polish on it'.
(See also **Clichés**.)

282 Singular or plural?
A. (i) Certain nouns ending in 's' (*ethics, economics, physics,
mathematics, genetics*) take a singular verb when considered as a
subject.
*Examples: Economics **is** taken by most students of Commerce.*
        *Physics **is** her favourite subject.*
        *Mathematics **was** always a difficult subject for me.*
But considered from a slightly different viewpoint, some of these
nouns require a plural verb.
Example (a) In the example given above, 'Economics' refers to a
        subject or field of study, and a singular verb is required.
        But in the sentence, 'The economics of the situation
        have to be considered', the reference is to certain factors
        which are relevant to the situation, such as consider-
        ations of supply and demand, and effects on prices and
        employment. In this case the plural verb 'have' is
        correct.
Example (b) *My mathematics **are** weak.* This sentence suggests that
        the speaker is thinking not of one whole field of study
        but of various mathematical processes which he has

105

failed to master. In this case the plural verb 'are' is correct.

Similarly the following sentences suggest that the speaker has in mind the qualities, beliefs or policies that characterize a particular person's politics or ethics.

*His politics **are** of the far right.*

*Such ethics **are** deplorable.*

(ii) In a sentence such as, 'It **is** the children who suffer most', the subject (it) is always singular even though the following complement (the children) may be plural. Another example is, 'It **was** the younger men who caused the disturbance'.

When a complement is qualified by an adjective clause introduced by a relative pronoun (who, which, that) the verb in this adjective clause agrees in number with the complement.

*Examples: It is your **manners** that **have** lost us many supporters.*

*It is **John and Mary** who **are** to blame for this confusion.*

(iii) Sometimes a subject consists of a whole clause beginning with 'what'.

*Examples: **What caused the confusion** (was, were) two cars which had broken down.*

***What the crowd enjoyed most** (was, were) the juggling acts.*

In each of these sentences, 'it' can be substituted for the subject, indicating that the sense is singular and that the singular verb 'was' is required.

On the other hand, the plural verb is required in, 'What appeared to be clumps of palm trees **were** really mirages', because 'what' clearly relates to the plural noun 'mirages'.

(iv) When 'number of' means 'more than one', it has a plural sense and so takes a plural verb.

*Example: A **number** of parents **were** in the school-ground.*

But when 'number of' means 'total' the sense, and the verb, are singular.

*Example: The **number** of spectators **was** a record.*

B. (i) 'More than one . . .' is used in association with a singular verb.

*Examples: There **is** more than one cause contributing to this accident.*

*More than one criminal **was** involved in the theft.*

(ii) Some plural nouns name a single quantity, and therefore take singular verbs.

*Examples: Two miles **is** too long for a junior event.*

*Fifty pounds **was** a rather heavy fine.*

(iii) In these sentences the subject word is 'one', and this requires a singular verb.

Examples: ***One*** *of the rings* ***was*** *missing.*
       One *of these coats* ***is*** *mine.*

(iv) (*a*) *This is one of the cars that was damaged in the accident.* This sentence is incorrect; 'that' refers to 'cars' which is a plural noun requiring the plural verb 'were', thus, '. . . one of the cars that **were** damaged . . .'

    (*b*) *She is one of those people who is always untidy.* This is wrong; amend it to '. . . people who **are** always untidy.'

    (*c*) *One of the buildings that* ***is*** *of special interest is the old court-house.* This is correct; the clause introduced by 'that' refers to 'one' building and so requires the singular verb 'is'.

(See also **Agreement, Collective noun, Either, Everyone,** and **There is.**)

283 Slang

People use slang because of its novelty, and the desire for novelty ensures that most slang terms have a short, overworked existence. But some slang words are very appropriate and expressive; these remain longer in use, and a few of them are absorbed into the language. Examples of slang terms that have become respectable are: *barracker, hitch-hiker, gadget, dole, stunt.*

Slang is more readily accepted in conversation than in writing. It should be avoided in formal writing if there is a standard word that is appropriate. If it is found necessary or desirable to use a slang term, it should be written in quotation marks. This suggests that you are saying, 'I know this is slang, but I find it the best word to express what I have in mind'.

284 So

A clause stating purpose is introduced by the words 'so that', not by 'so as' or by 'so' alone.

Example: Ted hurried to finish his work ***so that*** *he could go fishing with Frank.*

'So' by itself cannot be used as a conjunction. Add 'and'.

Example: It is raining today and so we decided to stay at home.

285 Sort. See **Kind**

286 Spelling

A weak speller who wishes to improve his spelling must make a systematic attack on the problem. Teachers and members of his family can help by joining in word games and spelling activities. And some textbooks provide useful exercises. But the **learning** always remains the task of the student. One day perhaps, a reform of our spelling will reduce the magnitude of this difficult task.

A. (i) Keep a list of words that are found to be confusing. Write them in phrases, *for example, crossed the* **border**, *Mrs Brown's two* **boarders**; **coarse** *sugar, the race-***course**; **hoped** *to hear,* **hoping** *to hear; a* **site** *for a house. weak eye-***sight**.

(ii) Difficult parts of words may be emphasized by underlining, *for example, noticeable, changeable, business, parallel, address.*

(iii) Arrange words in groups that are meaningful to you.

Examples: 'ful' words: *mouthful, spoonful, cupful, bucketful, armful;*
          silent letters: *sign, reign, sigh, knowledge;*
          'ei' after 'c': *receive, deceive, receipt, deceit;*
          'ie' words: *believe, relieve, thief, niece;*
          inconsistent groups:
          (a) same letters, different sounds—
             rough, cough, though, tough, dough;
          (b) same sound, different letters—
             receive, believe, key, fleece, peace.

(iv) Look over your lists of words often. Write some of them in new phrases or sentences, and ask somebody to check these.

B. (i) Try to develop the skill of using a dictionary effectively. Remember that a dictionary gives you not only the meaning and spelling, but also the correct pronunciation which is essential to correct spelling.

Unfortunately there are two serious difficulties involved in learning to use the dictionary.

(a) A weak speller, although aware of his general weakness, is usually not aware that he is about to spell a particular word wrongly, and therefore has no incentive to consult a dictionary.

(b) Because of his imperfect knowledge of letter combinations and the sounds they represent, a poor speller may have difficulty in finding words to check their spelling. For example, it may not occur to him to look under the letter 'p' to find the words, 'physics', 'psychology', or 'pneumonia'.

The assistance of a teacher or a friend who is a good speller will help to overcome these difficulties.

(ii) Make intelligent use of a textbook which explains the rules of spelling. Mastery of **all** the rules and the exceptions is difficult, but some useful rules are quite simple. Often rules can be simplified to help with a person's particular spelling problems.

The four rules that follow are examples of simplified rules which apply to groups of words that are frequently mis-spelt.

(a) **-ceed**, **-cede**, or **-sede**

Only one word ends '-sede': *supersede.*

Only three words end '-ceed': *succeed, proceed, exceed.*

All other words with this final sound end '-cede', *for example, precede, concede, cede, accede, recede.*

(b) **ei** or **ie** to represent the sound 'ee'

The rule is, 'ei' after 'c', 'ie' after other letters.

Examples: receive, deceive, receipt, conceit, conceive;
believe, niece, achieve, pierce, brief.

Exceptions: seize, weir, weird, protein.

For sounds other than 'ee', write 'ei', *for example, weight, height, skein, leisure, forfeit, neighbour.*

(c) Doubling a final consonant

When adding '-ed', '-er', or '-ing', double a final consonant in **one-syllable words** in which the final consonant is preceded by **one vowel**.

Examples: hop, hopped, hopping;
tan, tanned, tanner;
fit, fitting, fitter.

two- or multi-syllable words stressed on the **last syllable**, when the final consonant is preceded by **one vowel**.

Examples: prefer, preferred;
allot, allotted;
commit, committed, committing;
control, controller.

(d) Final 'e'—retained or dropped?

Drop 'e' before adding a syllable beginning with a **vowel**.

Examples: love, lovable, loving;
wave, waving;
advise, advisable;
desire, desirous.

Exceptions: final 'e' is **retained in certain words after a soft 'c'** or **soft 'g'**.

Examples: change, changeable;
service, serviceable;
notice, noticeable;
courage, courageous.

Retain 'e' if the syllable added begins with a **consonant**.

Examples: care, careless, careful;

109

> *vague, vaguely;*
> *encourage, encouragement.*

Correct spelling is a convention which society still observes. Weak spelling does not lessen your worth as a person, but it may handicap you socially and in certain types of employment, such as journalism, teaching, and secretarial work. If you have talent, the world will not regard your spelling errors very seriously. Nevertheless, 'original' spelling will generally cause amusement rather than compel admiration.

C. Some common words that are frequently mis-spelt

abscess	calendar	eccentric	fourth
accelerate	cancel	ecstasy	fulfil
accessible	cancelled	edible	fulfilled
accidentally	cancellation	eighth	
accommodation	career	electricity	gaiety
acquaintance	catalogue	eligible	gauge
address	celery	embarrass	government
advertisement	cemetery	employee	grateful
adviser	changeable	enrol	guarantee
alignment	coconut	enrolled	
allot	coincidence	enrolment	harass
allotted	colossal	evaporate	humorous
amateur	commit	exaggerate	
anaesthetic	committed	excitement	illegible
apology	committee	excitable	immovable
appendicitis	connoisseur	excel	incidentally
argument	conscience	excellent	incinerator
asphalt	conscientious	existence	incredible
asthma	conscious	extremely	independent
audience	contemporary		initials
awful		fascinating	initialled
	definite(ly)	February	inoculate
bachelor	desirable	flexible	instalment
battalion	diary	fluorescent	invitation
benefited	disappear	focus	irresistible
biscuit	disappointed	focused	
breath (noun)	disastrous	forbid	jewellery
bronchitis	discipline	forty	jewels
burglar	dissatisfied	foul (play)	
business	doesn't	fourteen	label

labelled	occurrence	refer	souvenir
laboratory	omelette	referred	stony
lacquer	omit	reference	subtle
leisure	omitted	relevant	surely
library	omission	restaurant	
lilies		reversible	terrific
liquor	parallel	rheumatism	truly
	paralyse	rhyme	
mileage	parliament	rhythm	unnecessary
mischievous	persuade		until
myth	possess	sandwich	
	prefer	satellite	vaccinate
necessary	preferable	scarce	vehicle
niece	preference	scarcely	vertical
nineteen	preferred	scenery	
ninety	privilege	secretary	weather (fine)
ninth	professor	seize	Wednesday
noticeable	psychology	separate	weird
	punctual	serviceable	wilful
oblige	pursue	severely	woollen
occasionally		similar	
occur	queue	sincerely	
occurred		skilful	

Note: Separate entries explain the use of some word pairs. See
Dependant, Dependent; **Lose, Loose**: **Practice, Practise**; **Principal,
Principle**; and **Stationary, Stationery**.

287 Split infinitive
An infinitive, which usually consists of a verb preceded by the word
'to' (*to run, to try, to eat*) is 'split' when an adverb or a phrase is
inserted between 'to' and the verb.
Examples: (a) *The pupils were told* **to quickly put** *their books away.*
　　　　　(b) *I want you* **to thoroughly wash** *these instruments.*
Splitting an infinitive should be avoided whenever possible, and
splitting with anything more than one word should be avoided
always. In the examples given, it is better to write (a) as '. . . to put
their books away quickly.' and (b) as '. . . to wash these instruments
thoroughly'.
However, splitting an infinitive is sometimes desirable in order to
avoid writing an awkward or ambiguous sentence. In the following
sentences the split infinitives are justified.

111

Examples: *He seemed determined* **to really enjoy** *himself.*

        The guards could be trusted **to stoutly defend** *the castle.*

        To deliberately avoid *a split infinitive is* **to sometimes write** *unnatural English.*

Consider the following sentences, and decide whether the split infinitive in sentence (*c*) conveys a different shade of meaning and is therefore justified.

(*a*) *The detective said it is difficult always to catch your man.*

(*b*) *The detective said it is difficult to catch your man always.*

(*c*) *The detective said it is difficult to always catch your man.*

(See also **Infinitive**.)

288 Spoiled, Spoilt

(i) When the meaning is 'damaged or impaired to some extent', 'spoiled' is generally preferred. When the sense is 'ruined'—that is, when the spoiling is complete—the tendency is to use 'spoilt'.

Examples: *The cool wind* **spoiled** *our swimming carnival.*

        A number of minor errors have **spoiled** *your essay.*

        The cake was burnt so badly that it was completely **spoilt**.

(ii) When the function is adjectival, 'spoilt' is generally used, *for example, a* **spoilt** *child, a* **spoilt** *dinner, a* **spoilt** *voting form.*

289 Stationary, Stationery

'Stationary' is an adjective meaning 'motionless', *for example, a stationary train.*

'Stationery' is a noun, meaning 'writing material', *for example, envelopes and other stationery.*

290 Stimulant, Stimulus

A **stimulus** is an incentive. A **stimulant** is something taken to improve the functioning of some part of the body or to induce a feeling of well-being.

Examples: *A reduction in taxation is usually a* **stimulus** *to trade.*

        Coffee and tea are mild **stimulants**.

291 Stop, Stay

'Stop' is used when the reference is to ceasing an action such as moving or talking.

Examples: *Does this train* **stop** *at Bordertown?*

        The pupils were told to **stop** *talking.*

'Stay' is used when the sense is 'remain'.

*Examples: I hope to **stay** in Rome for a few days.*
    ***Stay** there until I bring a ladder.*
'Stop' is also used when the sense is to stay for a stated or implied period of time.
*Example: The bus **stops** at Windsor for an hour so that we can see the castle.*

292 Style (A)—The need for clarity

Style is determined by the personality of the writer, rather than by his grasp of principles of composition and rules of grammar. Nevertheless, all writers except the very few in whom unorthodox attitudes combine successfully with great talent, must go some way towards observing the conventions of writing.

Nearly all writing is intended to be read, and this requires that it be presented in language acceptable to and intelligible to readers. Language like money, is a medium of exchange—in this case the exchange of ideas—and must be acceptable to both the writer who offers and the reader who receives the ideas.

Long technical words in complicated sentences tend to make reading difficult. *Some* technical words may be needed in professional material, but outside the pages of an advanced textbook, simple, precise language used as concisely as possible is almost always the easiest to read and the most acceptable as good style.

293 Style (B)—Cultivating a good style

(i) To develop a good writing style three things are necessary:

(a) the **talent** to write;

(b) **practice** to develop your talent;

(c) **reading** of the works of good authors to refine your talent.

(ii) Each **paragraph** you write should deal with one aspect of your subject and should fit logically into your plan for covering the subject. (You will have jotted down several paragraph headings before you started writing.) The length of a paragraph should reflect its importance to the whole discussion. In most cases your final paragraph will be brief, summing up, or expressing your final thought on the subject.

(iii) Each **sentence** should contribute a relevant idea, expressed concisely and clearly. Transition from idea to idea, and from one paragraph to another, should be smooth. This quality of smoothness depends largely on (a) variety in the length and the construction of your sentences, and (b) your ability to use effectively the connector words and phrases, such as: *In addition . . . , Nevertheless . . . , Moreover . . . , However . . . , Meanwhile . . . , For this reason . . . ,*

113

In contrast to . . . , On the other hand . . . , On the contrary . . . .
(iv) Devices, such as, comparisons, contrasts, and examples, should be used judiciously to give emphasis to selected points. Your language should be simple, concrete, restrained, free of fancy words, and precise, so that it expresses your meaning exactly and sincerely.
(v) Always re-read what you have written, with the intention of correcting errors and improving passages that do not satisfy you.
(vi) For other hints on style, see **Sentence—Qualities; Unity; Coherence; Circumlocution; Redundancy; Tautology; Ambiguity; Abstract and concrete language; Clichés; Jargon; Journalese; Euphemism; Euphony; Neologisms; Slang; Metaphor; Synonyms; Shades of meaning; Simile.**

294 Subconscious, Unconscious

'Unconscious' means 'not aware of one's feelings or surroundings'. 'Subconscious' refers to impressions made upon the mind of which we are not aware. The subconscious mind influences our thoughts and conduct, and is related to our dreams.
*Examples: The injured driver was **unconscious** for several hours.*
*The working of the **subconscious** mind often causes strange dreams.*

295 Subsequent, Consequent

(i) The word 'subsequent' indicates that one event comes after another. 'Consequent' implies that the second event follows as a result or consequence of the first.
*Examples: The opening ceremony was colourful, but the **subsequent** proceedings were boring.*
*About noon a riot broke out, and in the **consequent** confusion I was able to escape.*
(ii) The prepositions that follow 'subsequent' and 'consequent' are 'to' and 'on' (or 'upon') respectively.
*Examples: The rise in the accident rate, **subsequent to** the installation of new machinery, puzzled the manager.*
*The unrest among the workers **consequent upon** the introduction of faster production schedules did not surprise the union officials.*

296 Such

(i) *Some of our neighbours keep a number of goats such as Mr Brown.*
Errors of this kind are avoided by taking care to place 'such as' immediately after the word it qualifies. *Some of our neighbours, such*

as Mr Brown, keep a number of goats.
(ii) *The meeting was attended by labourers, shop assistants, waitresses, and such like.* 'Such like' or 'and the like' are vulgarisms to be avoided.
(iii) Avoid using 'such' as a pronoun in expressions like 'if such is the case'. It is better to use 'this' or 'that'.

297 Summon, Summons

(i) 'Summons' may be used as (a) a noun and (b) a verb.
(a) A person receives a **summons** from the legal authorities, demanding his attendance before a court at a stated time.
(b) As a verb also, 'summons' is used in the judicial sense, as in 'After the accident the other driver threatened to **summons** me', that is, '. . . have a **summons** to court served on me'.
(ii) When the meaning is 'order or request' (verb), the correct word is the verb 'summon'.
*Examples: The King decided to **summon** all his advisers to a special meeting.*
*I am **summoned** to appear at the inquiry next Monday.*
*While we were chatting, Jones was **summoned** to the telephone.*

298 Synonyms

Synonyms are words of similar meaning. It has been said that there are no true synonyms in English. Certainly there are few, for few words mean exactly the same as another word, or are equally appropriate in all contexts. There are many words that are similar in their general meaning, but they are distinguished from one another by shades of meaning, and are not always interchangeable. For example, 'monstrous', 'vast', 'gigantic', 'prodigious', and 'astronomical' all convey the idea of great size, but each has its own shade of meaning making it more suitable than the others in a given context. There are other words close enough in meaning to be interchangeable in many contexts—'huge', 'enormous', 'immense', and 'colossal'. A careful writer takes the trouble to use the right word, that is, the most precise and expressive in the particular context.
For each of the following groups of words, consider (i) the general meaning of the group, and (ii) the shade of meaning which each word has and which is not expressed by other words in the group.
(*a*) *friend, ally, accomplice, colleague, collaborator*
(*b*) *alien, exile, refugee, immigrant*
(*c*) *abandon, desert, relinquish, recant, abdicate*
(See also **Shades of meaning**.)

115

T

299 Tautology

Tautology is the needless repetition of an idea in different words. One has to be alert indeed to avoid tautology at all times. We often hear sentences such as, 'There were many different kinds of flowers in the show'. Is the word 'different' necessary here? Is it not implied in the word 'kinds'?

In the sentence, 'The length of the wire is too short to mend the fence', are the first three words necessary?

Other examples: equally as good as;
the important essentials;
the modern car of today;
the end result;
refer back to;
purple in colour;
circular in shape;
tried in vain . . . but failed;
subsequently followed.

(See also **Redundancy**.)

300 Tense

A. Most verbs express actions. The inflections or changed forms of a verb that indicate time of the action are called 'tenses' of the verb (from Latin, *tempus* meaning time). There are a number of tense forms but they all come under three general headings—**present, past, and future**. Perfect tense is a form which refers to an action completed in the present, the past, or the future.

(See also **Perfect tense**.)

Examples: **Present** tense: *I eat. I am eating.*
Past tense: *I ate. I was eating.*
Future tense: *I shall eat.*
Perfect tense: *I have eaten.*

The following **tense forms are the source of many errors**. Practise these correct forms by using them to construct sentences.

116

Present tense	Past tense	Perfect tense
I run.	*I ran.*	*I have run. He has run.*
I see.	*I saw.*	*I have seen. She has seen.*
I do.	*I did.*	*I have done. Have I done?*
I go.	*I went.*	*I have gone. Has he gone?*
I come.	*I came.*	*I have come. It has come.*
I ring.	*I rang.*	*I have rung.*
I swim.	*I swam.*	*I have swum.*
I drink.	*I drank.*	*I have drunk.*
I sing.	*I sang.*	*I have sung.*
Birds fly.	*The birds flew.*	*The birds have flown.*
Water flows.	*The water flowed.*	*The water has flowed.*

B. (i) Inconsistency in the use of tenses should be avoided. In most cases a sentence begun in a certain tense should be completed in that tense. The sentences in the following examples **break this rule**.

Examples: *We **crept** up and, hiding behind a stack of boxes, we **watch** the thieves trying to open the safe.* (Correct by changing present tense 'watch' to past tense 'watched' which is consistent with 'crept'.)

*If we **knew** the code we **can** read the message.* (Change 'can' to 'could' to be consistent with past tense 'knew'.)

*They **boasted** as if they **have** already **won** the match.* (The past perfect 'had . . . won' is required after the past tense 'boasted'.)

(ii) The use of different tenses in one sentence is not always wrong. The following sentences are **correct**.

Examples: *We **shall** soon **know** whether he **is** reliable.* (Future tense followed by present tense to express a **continuing fact**.)

*Columbus **said** that the earth **is** round.* (Past tense followed by present tense to express a **universal fact**.)

301 Than

(i) When a pronoun is used after 'than', it is best to supply the understood but missing words, in order to decide which pronoun is correct.

Examples: *You can run faster than **I** (can).*

*My dog seems to like you better than (he likes) **me**.*

*You trust him more than **I** (do).*

*You trust him more than (you trust) **me**.*

(ii) *Fruit is cheaper this season **than what** it was last year.* In sentences such as this, 'what' is unnecessary and should be omitted.

117

302 That

'That' should not be used as an adverb of degree instead of 'so'.
*Incorrect: I was **that** tired I fell asleep.*
*Correct: I was **so** tired that I fell asleep.*

303 The (the definite article)

(i) When two nouns are joined by 'and', care must be taken to include the article 'the' when the sense requires it. Note in the following pairs of sentences the difference in meaning that depends on the inclusion or omission of 'the'.
Examples: The black and white cows have been sold.
The black and the white cows have been sold.

The Secretary and Treasurer has not yet arrived. (one person)
The Secretary and the Treasurer have not yet arrived. (two persons)

(ii) If the two nouns are thought of in association, the article need not be repeated if there is no risk of confusion.
Example: The Duke and Duchess of Windsor lived in America.
But the article is clearly required in the sentence, 'The King and the Duke of Edinburgh visited the hospital'.
We may say, 'The Republicans and Democrats will unite to fight this evil'; but when the combination follows 'both' the article is required, 'Both the Republicans and the Democrats will fight this evil'.
The article is also repeated when an alternative is indicated by 'or'.
Example: Do you prefer the blue or the green car?

304 There, Their, They're

'There' means 'at that place'; 'their' means 'belonging to them'; 'they're' means 'they are'.
*Examples: Put the parcel over **there**. **There** is plenty of room.*
*Have you visited **their** home?*
*I shall return these eggs to the grocer; **they're** all cracked.*

305 There is

In the sentence, 'There are four lorries to be loaded', the subject is 'four lorries'. The verb 'are' is plural, in agreement with 'four lorries'. But a singular verb is used if a plural noun denotes a single amount or unit.

118

Examples: **There is** *five pounds to pay to clear this debt.*
There's *only a few handfuls of rice left.*
There is *eggs and bacon for breakfast.*
There was *much laughing and joking at the party.*
Have you room for all of us? **There's** *John, Fred, Anne and myself.*

306 Think

'Think' should **not** be used as an equivalent of 'remember', as in 'Did you think to switch off the television set?'
It is more acceptable when 'Did you think . . .' means, 'Did the thought enter your head . . .' or 'Did it occur to you . . . .'
Examples: **Did you think** *to ask whether the landlady supplies the linen?*
I didn't **think** *to ask the postman whether he had seen my dog.*

307 Thus

(i) 'Thus' means 'in this way' or 'by this means'. When it is used with a following participle care must be taken to see that the participle is not related to the wrong noun or pronoun.
Incorrect: *The detective's car was stolen,* **thus** *causing him much embarrassment.* (In this sentence 'causing' refers to 'car', and the meaning expressed—that the car caused embarrassment—is not the meaning intended.)
Correct: *The detective's car was stolen, and this caused him much embarrassment.*
Thieves stole the detective's car, **thus** *causing him much embarrassment.*
(ii) *The lava flowed slowly down the mountain-side,* (*thus*) *destroying everything in its path.* In this sentence 'thus' confuses the meaning, and should be omitted.
(See also **'Dangling' (unrelated) constructions**.)

308 Titles

(i) In writing the titles of books and literary works, it is customary to use either single inverted commas or underlining. The two methods should not be used together, although they may be used in the same sentence.
Examples: C. J. Dennis's poem, 'Joi, the Glug', was published in The

Glugs of Gosh.

'Romeo and Juliet' is available in the copy of Shakespeare's Complete Works in the library.

(ii) In print, titles may be underlined, placed in single inverted commas, or set in italics.

(iii) Original titles (such as the heading to an essay) or transferred titles (such as songs listed as items in a programme) should be written without inverted commas.

(iv) As a general rule, the articles 'A'. 'An', and 'The' should be included in the titles of books, plays, poems, etc. Often, sound or general effect influences a writer to include or omit the article. Omission of 'The' causes no awkwardness in referring to Russell's 'Principles of Mathematics', but the article must surely be included in a reference to T. F. Powys's 'The Left Leg.'.

(v) Some printers ignore certain details, such as the apostrophe to indicate possessive case, in setting headings and titles.

309 To, Too, Two

*Examples: It is **too** hot **to** walk **two** miles.*
*I am going **to** Wales for **two** months; John is coming **too**.*

310 Try

'Try to win' is preferable to 'try and win'. However, use of the latter may be justified when it is desired to express determination.

U

311 Undue, Unduly

These two words are often confused. This confusion can be avoided by using other, more precise words. The following sentences illustrate the correct use of the two words.

Examples: (*a*) *He is **unduly** optimistic about his chances of winning the lottery.* (i.e. **unreasonably** optimistic)
*She became **unduly** excited about the visitors' arrival.*
(*b*) *The judge showed **undue** harshness in sentencing the prisoner.* (i.e. misplaced or unjustifiable sternness)
*The mother showed **undue** concern for the child who arrived home late.*

Do not use 'unduly' in the sense of 'excessively' in sentences such as: *That coat is not unduly expensive.*
I was not driving unduly fast.

Avoid too, the unnecessary use of 'undue' as in, 'There is no cause for undue alarm' (or undue pessimism). The meaning of 'undue' is already expressed in the words 'no cause for'.

312 Uninterested. See Disinterested

313 Unique

A thing that is unique is one that has no like or equal. A thing cannot be 'rather unique', or 'more unique'.
(See also **Comparison of adjectives**.)
'Perfect' is another idea that cannot be expressed in degrees. A thing is either perfect or imperfect; it can be nearer to perfection than another thing, but not 'fairly perfect' or 'more perfect'.

314 Unity

A sentence should be clear and coherent, but it is unlikely to have either of these qualities unless it has **unity**. A sentence has unity when all the thoughts expressed in it are associated, contributing to the same general idea. The following sentences break the law of unity and consequently are not entirely sensible.

Examples: Nero played the fiddle while Rome burnt and persecuted his opponents.

Henry VIII had six wives and an ulcer on his leg.

He is the manager of our local bank and breeds tropical fish.

Sometimes the thoughts in a badly written sentence cannot be successfully related, and must be re-stated in separate sentences. In other cases, as in the third example above, rewriting can produce a satisfactory sentence.

Example: He is the manager of our local bank and, as a hobby, breeds tropical fish.

315 Unrelated participle. See 'Dangling' (unrelated) constructions

316 Unsatisfied, Dissatisfied

'Unsatisfied' is used when some need or desire has not been fully provided, 'dissatisfied' when the meaning is 'discontented'.

*Examples: Even after the large meal the boy's hunger was **unsatisfied**. In spite of their good wages the workers remained **dissatisfied**.*

317 Use of dictionary

All students know that a dictionary gives the meanings of words. But many do not realize what a wealth of other information is contained in a good dictionary.

It is sensible for a student to have a good *small* dictionary to carry or to have on the desk for the checking of everyday spellings; a good *large* dictionary should be available in every library and wherever else students congregate to work. Very tiny dictionaries, although easy to carry, are rarely useful because of their small word coverage.

The questions following are included to direct your attention to the dictionary's many uses.

(a) What is a fandango?

(b) Who are the *hoi polloi*?

(c) What are two different meanings of the word 'fallow'?

(d) What is the correct pronunciation of: compensatory, patio, exquisite, comparable?

(e) From what languages did English borrow the words 'slogan' and 'motto', 'plunder' and 'ransack'?

(f) What is the meaning of 'plagiarism', and what was its origin or derivation?

(g) Suggest two words similar in meaning to 'defective'.

(h) Why is a certain type of woollen jacket called a 'cardigan'?

(i) Who ate the first sandwich?

(j) What have the words 'pendant', 'pendulum', and 'appendix' in common?

(k) Are 'judgment' and 'judgement' recognized alternative spellings?

(l) What is the noun corresponding to the adjective 'notorious'?

(m) Is 'dollar' an American word?

(n) Give two idioms or colloquial expressions which include the word 'jack'.

(o) What is a man speaking about when he refers to his *'alma mater'*?

(p) Is a 'caret' the same as a 'carat'?

V

318 Verb

A. (i) A verb is a word which expresses an action or a state of being.

Examples: verbs expressing action: *eats, laughed, wrote, dig*

verbs expressing state of being: *is, am, are, was, were, become, seem*

Every complete sentence has a verb, but in some sentences the verb is understood, and not written, as in '(I **am**) Present, sir'.

(ii) Many verbs consist of more than one word.

*Examples: Tom **is eating** his lunch.*

*Fay **has written** her essay.*

*I **shall finish** this work on time.*

In each of these sentences, the verb is made up of a **part-verb** (eating, written, finish) together with an **auxiliary** verb, sometimes called a 'helper' verb.

The most common **auxiliary** verbs are

(*a*) *shall, will, would, should, may, might, must, can, could;*

(*b*) parts of the verb 'to be': *is, am, are, was, were;*

(*c*) parts of the verb 'to have': *have, has, had.*

Part-verbs include

present participles: *running, eating, laughing, trying;*

past participles: *eaten, broken, swum, done, begun;*

infinitives: *to go, to eat, to swim, to begin, to try.*

A participle or an infinitive is not a verb but a part-verb. A participle may be combined with an auxiliary to form a complete verb.

*Examples: He **was laughing** loudly.*

*I **am trying** to solve this puzzle.*

*The tree **has fallen** across the road.*

***Have** you **eaten** your lunch?*

B. One of the most common causes of incorrect usage is a **confusion concerning the past tense and the past participle** of certain verbs.

For practice in correct usage, construct sentences using the following verbs. The first of each pair is the past tense, the second consists of an auxiliary verb combined with the past participle.

*Example: A rabbit **ate** my lettuces.*

*A rabbit **has eaten** my lettuces.*

ate, has eaten; fell, has fallen; saw, have seen; did, have done; saw, was seen; came, has come; went, have gone; ran, has run; rang, has rung; swam, have swum; rose, has risen; sank, has sunk; blew, has blown; flew, have flown; broke, has broken; began, have begun; drank, has drunk; wrote, have written; sang, have sung; chose, has chosen; drew, has drawn; showed, has shown; threw, has thrown; flowed, has flowed.

319 Very, Much

(i) When a past participle is used as an adjective it is preceded by 'very'.

*Examples: John is **very** interested in gemstones.*

*I am **very** pleased to see you again.*

(ii) When the participle retains its verbal function it is preceded by 'much' (or 'very much').

*Examples: Heysen's paintings are **much** admired.*

*His business methods are **much** criticized.*

*He was **very much** offended by your remark.*

(iii) It is sometimes difficult to decide which word—'very' or 'much' —should precede a participle. The rules stated in (i) and (ii) are general rules which are not applicable in all cases. When in doubt use the word which sounds natural in the sentence you are writing.

320 Via

'Via' means 'by way of' and is used in reference to a route.

*Example: We travelled from Sydney to New York **via** Honolulu and Los Angeles.*

'Via' should **not** be used to refer to a method of transport, as in '. . . London to Paris via British Airways'.

In this case, 'by' takes the place of 'via'.

321 View

(i) The phrase 'in view of', followed by a noun, expresses reason.

*Example: **With a view to** easing the unemployment in rural areas, the government will initiate a programme of public works.*

(ii) The phrase 'with a view to' expresses purpose.

*Example: **With a view to** easing the unemployment in rural areas, the government will initiate a programme of public works.*

(iii) It is a common error to use an infinitive after 'with a view'; the gerund (ending -ing) should be used instead of the infinitive.

*Incorrect: He has commenced a university course, **with a view** to become a teacher.*

Correct: ... *course,* **with a view** to **becoming** *a teacher.*

322 Voice

The term 'voice' refers to the form of the verb which indicates whether the subject of a sentence **acts** or is **acted upon**.

A verb is in the **active voice** when the person or thing named by the **subject performs** the action.

*Examples: A **dog chased** the boy.*
*Our **forward kicked** three goals.*
***Tom caught** four fish.*

A verb is in the **passive voice** when the person or thing named by the **subject suffers** the action.

*Examples: The **boy was chased** by a dog.*
*Three **goals were kicked** by our forward.*
*Four **fish were caught** by Tom.*

In writing, the active and passive forms of the verb should be mixed, with the active voice predominating because it is more direct and adds vigour, especially in narrative passages.

323 Voluntary, Voluntarily

'Voluntary' is an adjective, used before a noun.

*Example: Our club is maintained by **voluntary** labour.* (or ***voluntary** contributions*)

'Voluntarily' is an adverb, used to modify a verb.

*Examples: The escaped prisoner **voluntarily** gave himself up to the police.*
*The committee members worked **voluntarily** every Saturday afternoon.*

W

324 Wait, Await

(i) These two words are not interchangeable. We wait for a friend or a bus; we **await** an event or a development.

*Examples: We have to **wait** half an hour for the next bus.*
*I **waited** till two o'clock but he didn't appear.*
*I **await** your decision with interest.*
*The students anxiously **awaited** publication of their examination results.*

(ii) 'Await' is also used when the sense is 'to be in store for'.

*Examples: They little thought what bad news **awaited** them at home.*
*Rich rewards **await** the man who finds a cure for the common cold.*

325 Waste, Wastage

'Waste' refers to things used unnecessarily, such as food, money, or electricity.

*Example: The landlady asked her boarders not to **waste** electricity.*

'Wastage' refers to losses through causes that seem to be unavoidable, or inseparable from a process.

*Example: There is a considerable **wastage** of power involved in the transmission of electricity over long distances.*

326 What

Take care to ensure that sentences beginning with 'what' are not ambiguous, that is, of uncertain meaning.

*Examples: **What** is he crying for?* (Is he crying for possession of something, or should the question be, 'Why is he crying'?)
***What** did you sell your house for?* (This could refer to the **reason** for selling the house, or to the **sum** received. Say either, 'Why did you sell . . .?' or 'What sum (or price) did you . . .?'

327 Whereabouts

'Whereabouts' takes a singular verb.

*Example: His whereabouts **is** unknown.*

127

328 Whether. See If

329 Which

(i) *That is the dog **which** chased me.* In this sentence, 'which' is used correctly as a relative pronoun; it introduces a subordinate (adjective) clause, and refers clearly to an antecedent or previous noun, 'dog'.

(ii) *I gave the dog a bone, which pleased the little boy.* This sentence is grammatically incorrect. It suggests that the bone pleased the little boy, when the sense makes it clear that it was the act of giving the bone which pleased him. However, the use of 'which' (meaning 'and this') to refer back to a whole clause is now widely accepted in speech, but not in formal writing.

(iii) If the relative pronoun 'which' is used to refer back to a whole clause, ambiguity may arise. Often it is better to recast the sentence. The correct placement of a comma can also clarify the meaning.

Incorrect: *I caught the mouse **which** pleased the girls.* (This says that the mouse pleased the girls.)

Correct: *I caught the mouse, **and** this pleased the girls.*

             *I caught the mouse, **which** pleased the girls.*

Note the possibility of confusing the meaning if the comma is omitted from the following sentences.

Examples: *The union officials criticized the strike, **which** pleased the manager.* (Did the strike please the manager?)

         *A power failure interrupted the rail services, **which** annoyed the public.* (Was it the rail services that annoyed the public?)

(See also **Which, What**.)

330 Which, What

A. 'Which' and 'what' are both used as interrogative adjectives (before a noun) and as interrogative pronouns (in place of a noun). Interrogative words are used to ask questions.

Examples: adjective use: ***What** bird is that?* ***Which** film did you prefer?*

         pronoun use: ***What** does he want?* ***Which** did he choose?*

'Which' is used when one knows the alternatives from which a choice is to be made.

Examples: ***Which** novel of Dickens did you enjoy most?*

         ***Which** of these toys would you like?*

Which train do you intend to travel on—the nine thirty, or the eleven fifteen?
Which restaurant shall we dine at—the Regal, or Antonio's?
These sentences suggest that the possible range of books, trains, toys, restaurants, is known.
(ii) 'What' is used when the situation is more vague, for example, when the basis of choice is not known.
Examples: What bird is that?
What presents did you receive on your birthday?
What restaurant did you dine at?
What train are you going by?
These sentences give no indication that a limited range of birds, presents, trains, restaurants, is known.
B. Care is needed when writing clauses beginning 'and which' and 'but which'. Such clauses should be added only after clauses which are of the same type and which refer to the same thing.
(i) *The house facing the beach and which is surrounded by a large lawn....* This is incorrect; 'and which' joins a phrase and a clause. Correct by changing the phrase to a clause: *The house **which** faces the beach **and which** is surrounded by a large lawn....*
(ii) *He bought a farm near a stream but which is too hilly to be irrigated.* Incorrect. Change the phrase 'near a stream' to match the clause introduced by 'but which': *He bought a farm **which** is near a stream **but which** is too hilly....*
(iii) Provided that the clauses co-ordinated by 'and which' or 'but which' are similar in type, the first need not begin with 'which'. The following sentence is correct: *He hopes to retire in the village where he lived as a boy and in which he owns several properties.*

331 Who, Whom

A. 'Who' is used as the **subject** and as the **complement** of a verb.
'Whom' is used as the **object** of a verb, and after a **preposition**.
*Examples: **Who** is there?* ('Who' is the subject of the verb 'is'.)
*   **Who** do you think he is?* ('Who' is complement of the verb 'is'. This is clearer if we rearrange the sentence—
You do think he is who?)
*   **Whom** did you see?* (*You did see whom?* 'Whom' is the object of the verb 'did see'.)
*   To **whom** are you writing?* ('Whom' is governed by the preposition 'to'.)
Nowadays when there is little objection to finishing a sentence with a preposition, sentences like the last one above are often introduced by 'who', although 'whom' is grammatically correct.

Examples: **Whom** *are you writing to?*
          Who *are you writing to?*

B. (i) *The man (who/whom), the police say, broke the window disappeared in the crowd.* Which pronoun—'who' or 'whom'—should be used in this sentence? The word required is the subject of the verb 'broke'; therefore the subject form 'who' is required: *The man* **who** *... broke the window . . . .* The addition of the clause 'the police say' does not alter the subject-verb relationship of the words 'who broke'.

(ii) *The boy (who/whom) we thought we had forgotten suddenly appeared.* In this sentence the word required is the object of the verb 'had forgotten'. The object form is 'whom': *The boy* **whom** *. . . we had forgotten . . . .*

(iii) It is a useful guide to substitute the pronoun 'he' or 'him' in such sentences. If 'he' (subject form) can be used, the subject form 'who' is correct. If 'him' (object form) can be substituted, the object form 'whom' is required. Thus in the sentences discussed we would say:

He *disappeared in the crowd.* (The subject form 'he' is used; therefore the subject form 'who' is correct.)

We had forgotten **him.** (The object form 'him' is used; therefore the object form 'whom' is required.)

332 Whose, Who's

'Whose' is a pronoun.

Examples: **Whose** *are these?*
          That is the boy **whose** *father repaired our car.*

'Who's' is a shortened form of 'who is'.

Example: **Who's** *coming swimming with me?*

333 Will, Would. See Shall, Should

334 With a view to

'With a view to' should be followed by a verb form ending in '-ing'.

Example: He bought the old home **with a view to repairing** *and selling it.*

(See also **View.**)

335 Without

(i) 'Without' should not be used as a substitute for 'unless', as in 'I cannot lift this without you help me'. There are two correct alternatives—either, 'I cannot . . . unless you help me', or 'I cannot . . . without your help'.

(ii) Avoid the absurd phrase, 'without hardly'.

Examples: (a) *The skier sped along without hardly touching the snow.*

(b) *We existed for a week without hardly a morsel of food.*

In (a) 'without' should be omitted; (b) can be corrected by saying '. . . with hardly a morsel . . . .'

336 With reference to

This phrase is indirect, and often clumsy. It is better to write simply and directly.

Examples: *With reference to your letter* . . . . ('**In reply to** your letter . . . .' is simpler, and effective.)

I am writing with reference to . . . . ('I am writing **about** . . . .' is better.)

337 Wonder

The following sentences are **statements**, not questions, and so do not require a question mark.

*I **wonder** why he did that.*

*I **wonder** whether they will arrive before lunch.*

338 Would have

Children and some older people, such as immigrants, who learn language through hearing rather than through reading, often learn to say 'would **of** tried' for 'would **have** tried'. This error results from the carelessness in speech of people who say something that sounds like 'would uv'. Needless to say, it is considered to be a very serious mistake in written English.

339 Wouldn't know

*There is no point in asking John; he **wouldn't know**.* This sentence is correct, but 'I wouldn't know' should not be used if the meaning is simply 'I do not know'.

Y

340 You and I, You and me

Many people believe that they should always say 'you and I', and
that 'you and me' is always wrong. Others believe that 'you and I' is
more refined and polite. Actually, both forms are correct in different
sentences.

(i) 'You and I' is correct when it forms the subject of a verb.

Examples: ***You and I agree** on this point.*

*Tom says that **you and I may go** in his car.*

(ii) 'You and me' is correct after a preposition, or when it is the
object of a verb.

Examples: *They were looking **at you and me.*** (after preposition 'at')

*Let Anne sit **between you and me.*** (after preposition
'between')

*That dog always **chases you and me.*** (object of the verb
'chases')

341 Your, You're, Yours

'Your' means 'belonging to you', *for example,* ***your** hat.*

'You're' means 'you are', *for example,* ***you're** late.*

Note that 'yours' is a possessive pronoun spelt without an apostrophe.
There is no apostrophe in '**Yours** faithfully', '**Yours** sincerely', or
'This pen is **yours**'.

Z

342 Zeugma

This is a figure of speech which combines the same verb with two very different and apparently unconnected objects. It should be used sparingly, but on occasion can produce a pleasantly humorous effect.

Examples: He lost his hat and his temper.
She put out the light and the cat before going to bed.

EXERCISES

The exercises are, with a few exceptions, of two types:

(i) Sentences which may be completed correctly by selecting an item from several items given in brackets. These exercises are introduced by the direction '*Select the correct item*'.

(ii) Sentences containing errors which are to be corrected. These exercises are introduced by the direction '*Write each sentence correctly*'.

Guidance in completing the exercises correctly is given in the Dictionary sections indicated. For example, in Exercise 3 (page 135), sentences (c) to (k) direct attention to guidance given in Section 10, sub-section B. on page 9.

Sets of exercises with 'A.' after the numbers (for example, **7. A.**) include additional practice exercises on important points of usage, and exercises that are more difficult.

1. Select the correct item.   Section
(a) The members elected (a, an) honorary secretary.   1
(b) I am studying for (a, an) M.A. degree.   1
(c) 'Your letter of the 16th ult . . .' refers to (this, next,
     last) month.   2
(d) The abbreviation q.v. means (please reply, see the
     reference mentioned, at your convenience).   2
(e) The prize was won by (Mr., Mr) (J. B., J B) Smith
     of Hawthorn.   2
(f) The manager (is'nt, isn't) in at present.   2
(g) The publisher has returned my (MS., M.S.)   2
(h) I listen regularly to the (B.B.C., BBC) news.   2
(i) (Subnormal, Abnormal) children require more care
     than the average child.   3
(j) The child was (subnormal, abnormal); she was born
     with only four toes on one foot.   3

2. Write each sentence correctly.   Section
(a) No nobler a man than Saint Francis has ever lived.   1
(b) Here is an interesting ad. for a new Jap. car.   2

(c) I trust that the above information will help you to
   make your decision.   4

(d) It is absolutely true that he has been to prison.   5

(e) Write more concrete versions of these sentences.   6

   (i) Every endeavour will be made to satisfy your requirements
       in regard to our product before the onset of upward vari-
       ations in price levels.

   (ii) Owing to the deterioration in my financial resources I found
        it an unavoidable necessity to reduce the frequency of my
        visits to places of theatrical entertainment.

   (iii) He was accompanied by a member of the fair sex whose
         facial characteristics were marred somewhat by auditory
         appendages of great dimensions.

3. Write each sentence correctly.   Section

(a) Our team won, but actually they were very lucky.   8

(b) This all adds up to the fact that we need to be
   cautious.   9

(c) We had a terrific time at the beach.   10 B.

(d) I left the smallest half of the cake for my brother.   10 B.

(e) Don't touch them grapes.   10 B.

(f) Please don't talk so loud in the library.   10 B.

(g) Jane is the most attractive of the twins.   10 B.

(h) Charles is much more cleverer than his brother John.   10 B.

(i) London is larger than any city in England.   10 B.

(j) We omitted the two last verses of the hymn.   10 B.

(k) The then government refused to increase pensions.   10 B.

4. Select the correct item.   Section

(a) My secretary will (inform you of, acquaint you
   with) my plans.   7

(b) The notice said, 'No (admittance, admission) except
   on business'.   11

(c) His (admittance, admission) that he was to blame for
   the accident shortened the enquiries made by the
   police.   11

(d) (Admittance, Admission) is one pound each.   11

(e) (Admittance, Admission) is by invitation only.   11

(f) He does not waste his (hard, hardly) earned cash.   13

(g) Mrs Smart always buys (high, highly) priced clothes.   13

(h) There is (a difference, no difference) between a new
   painted house and a newly-painted house.   13

135

(i) That foolish action is likely to aggravate (your
   injury, the old man, that savage dog).   16
(j) The citizens do not agree (to, with) the plan to build
   factories on the parkland.   17

5. Write each sentence correctly.   Section
(a) John writes very neat, don't you think?   12 B.
(b) Only park on this side of the street.   12 B.
(c) Ted was that tired he fell asleep in school.   12 B.
(d) I was that busy I never had no lunch today. (two
   errors)   12 B.
(e) A heap of weeds were blocking the gateway.   18 B.
(f) *Fathers and Sons* are one of the most popular novels
   about family relationships.   18 A.
(g) He complained all of the way to the picnic and all
   of the time we were there.   19
(h) We offer the best service; also our prices are lowest.   24
(i) Tom went with Frank to the shop, where he bought
   a knife.   26
(j) Don't kill your wife with hard work; let electricity
   do it.   26

6. Select the correct item.   Section
(a) I thanked him for giving me such sound (advice,
   advise).   14
(b) What did the lawyer (advice, advise) you to do?   14
(c) They say that (practice, practise) makes perfect.   14
(d) You should (practice, practise) every day to
   improve your playing.   14
(e) Have you a fishing (licence, license)?   14
(f) This shopkeeper is (licenced, licensed) to sell
   alcohol.   14
(g) The damp building (affected, effected) the children's
   health.   15
(h) Do frosts have any (affect, effect) on these plants?   15
(i) Are (all, all of) the nuts eaten? Yes, the children
   have eaten (all, all of) them.   19
(j) When the singers were (already, all ready) the
   conductor raised his baton to begin.   20
(k) He is only nineteen but (already, all ready) he has a
   university degree.   20

136

7. Select the correct item. | Section
(a) A cow and a horse (has, have) eaten my cabbages. | 18 A.
(b) A thief and murderer (has, have) escaped from custody. | 18 A.
(c) Whisky and soda (is, are) his favourite drink. | 18 A.
(d) Neither Tom nor Harry (has, have) finished (his, their) essay. | 18 B.
(e) *The Adventures of Tom Sawyer* (was, were) enjoyed by both the girls and the boys. | 18 A.
(f) Is Tom (alright, all right) again after his accident? | 21
(g) The police found the jewels (altogether, all together) in a cupboard. | 22
(h) The money seems to have disappeared (altogether, all together). | 22
(i) I (nearly, almost) offered to lend him my car. | 23
(j) I (nearly, almost) wish I had not accepted the money. | 23

7. A. Select the correct item. | Section
(a) He is (a, an) habitual drunkard. | 1
(b) The rain was (that, so) heavy all the streams were flooded. | 12 B.
(c) How often do you (practice, practise)? | 14
(d) The prisoner managed to (affect, effect) an escape in the darkness. | 15
(e) The (affect, effect) of his speech was to arouse the mob to violence. | 15
(f) Either Jane or Mary (is, are) at the door now. | 18

Write each sentence correctly.
(g) This course is the least of two evils. | 10 B.
(h) You must be hungry if you never had any lunch. | 12 B.
(i) If you don't write neater you'll have to repeat your work. | 13
(j) As I was departing from my place of domicile I was addressed by a mendicant whose raiment bore testimony to his condition of extreme destitution. | 6

8. Select the correct item. | Section
(a) He considered several (alternate, alternative) vocations before deciding to be a teacher. | 25
(b) The garrison had no (alternative, alternate) but to surrender. | 25

137

(c)	I have to serve in the shop and go to the market on (alternate, alternative) Fridays.	25
(d)	The two boys were helping (each other, one another) to build sand castles.	30
(e)	The caterers (anticipated, expected) a crowd of five thousand at the match, and increased their normal orders.	31
(f)	I (anticipate, expect) that he will win easily.	31
(g)	Please ask whether anybody forgot to bring (his, their) sleeping-bag.	33
(h)	(Anyone, Any one) could make an error of this kind.	33
(i)	(Anyone, Any one) of these knives is sharp enough.	33
(j)	Is it true that (your, you're) leaving town soon?	34
(k)	(Its, It's) true that I am leaving town soon.	34

9. Write each sentence correctly. — Section

(a)	A pot-plant was placed between each table.	27
(b)	He lost his knife amongst a stack of timber.	27
(c)	He is a man with many faults and who has many enemies.	28
(d)	The children spent Sunday at the beach. And enjoyed it very much.	28
(e)	The hibiscus is a flower of great beauty and which requires little attention.	29
(f)	Sydney is larger than any Australian city.	32
(g)	This pen was as expensive or more expensive than yours.	36
(h)	This pen was equally as expensive as yours.	36
(i)	Have you anything to say as to the cause of this damage?	40
(j)	Please let me have any information you possess as to his trouble with the police.	40

9. A. Write each sentence correctly. — Section

(a)	I am nearly glad that we did not win that contract.	23
(b)	Ted won the 220-yard event, also he was second in the high jump.	24
(c)	The witness told the judge he first saw the bandit as he entered the bank.	26
(d)	Wine should always be drunk with meals.	26
(e)	Now I want to mention two more pleasant subjects.	26

(f)	On arriving in London, his cousin met him at Waterloo Station.	26
(g)	The police watched the men from the farm-house.	26
(h)	I am looking for a secondhand car in sound mechanical order and which has had only one owner.	29
(i)	Explain the difference between: Supper is all ready on the table. Supper is already on the table.	20

10. Select the correct item.   Section

(a)	Did the committee (approve, approve of) your selection of prizes?	35
(b)	You must have these proposed alterations (approved, approved of) by the inspector of buildings.	35
(c)	She seems to like you as much as (I, me).	36
(d)	We rode (as, so) far as we could, and walked the rest of the way.	37
(e)	The excuses he gives are as (follow, follows).	38
(f)	Increased VAT must be paid (from, as from) last month, and higher income tax rates apply (from, as of) today.	39
(g)	The pupils, as well as the teacher, (was, were) interested in the drama.	41
(h)	The manager, as well as the employees, (was, were) concerned about the number of accidents.	41
(i)	The train strike affects you as well as (I, me).	41

10. A. Select the correct item.   Section

(a)	Toast and marmalade (is, are) a popular breakfast food.	18 A.
(b)	They seem to have forgotten us (altogether, all together).	22
(c)	The landing at Gallipoli incurred heavy casualties because the enemy had (expected, anticipated) it.	31
(d)	He pretends to like me as much as (she, her).	36
(e)	(As, So) far as I am concerned, he can do as he wishes.	37

Write each sentence correctly.

(f)	He said the government's policies would be absolutely disastrous.	5

(g) We believe this adds up to a threat to our interests.   9
(h) A large stack of container boxes were standing on
    the wharf.   18 B.
(i) Either he or you is to blame for this damage.   18 B.
(j) Is your car alright again after the repairs.?   21

11. Write each sentence correctly.   Section
(a) Jane seems awfully happy in her new job.   42
(b) I thought it was a frightful party.   42
(c) The swallows always come back again in the summer.   43
(d) The police searched back of the garage for the stolen
    goods.   44
(e) Barely had they entered the cave than an ominous
    rumbling was heard.   45
(f) No sooner had I taken my seat when there was a
    deafening crash.   45
(g) Why he overturned the car was because the brakes
    failed.   46
(h) Because a man is poor is no reason to think he is
    dishonest.   46
(i) I beg to inform you that we cannot supply the goods
    you require.   47
(j) This design is the best of the two.   49

11. A. Write each sentence correctly.   Section
(a) Ben Nevis is higher than any mountain in Scotland.   32
(b) Anyone in their right senses would not act so hastily.   33
(c) Anyone of these books deals with the subject you
    are studying.   33
(d) Please let me know whether your able to come.   34
(e) The reasons for the company's lower profit are as
    follow.   38
(f) I liked the traditional paintings, but as to the
    futuristic ones . . . !   40
(g) The officer, as well as the men, were surprised by
    the attack.   41
(h) The students, as well as the Principal was anxious to
    find the missing sporting equipment.   41
(i) These taxes will not affect you as much as I.   41
(j) Being a stranger in London, I was terribly pleased to
    see a face I knew.   42

12. Select the correct item.   Section

(a) The reason for Tom's failure is (that, because) he
    was over-confident.   46

(b) (Beside, Besides) all these business worries I have
    serious health problems.   48

(c) May the (better, best) man win!   49

(d) My grandfather's estate is to be shared between my
    cousin and (I, me).   50

(e) In former days only (*bona fides, bona fide*) travellers
    were served with liquor after trading hours.   51

(f) The (Webb brothers, brothers Webb) are popular
    entertainers.   54

(g) The bushfire (burnt, burned) for several days.   55

(h) The acid (burnt, burned) a hole in the carpet.   55

(i) 'Mr Jones, (can, may) I borrow your soldering
    iron?'
    'Certainly, Mr Smith, if we (may, can) find it.'   57

(j) I asked him if I (may, might) borrow his bicycle
    pump.   57

13. Write each sentence correctly.   Section

(a) You should leave a space of four feet between each
    shrub.   50

(b) I consider him both foolish, selfish and mean.   52

(c) James is both considerate to his parents and his
    grandparents.   52

(d) If I were a dictator which I am not I would send
    profiteers to prison.   53

(e) We never arrange a picnic but what it rains.   56

(f) I cannot help but smile.   56

(g) Have you read Mark Twain's book, the adventures
    of Huckleberry Finn?   58

(h) The bishop of Oxford is to preach at our church on
    Good Friday.   58

(i) I am sorry I cannot play squash tonight; I have a
    chronic cold.   62

(j) I now take up my pen to set down a few lines so that
    you may become acquainted with the sad fact that
    your good father's brother has unfortunately fallen
    into an unsatisfactory state of health.   64

14. Select the correct item.   Section
(a) (She, Her) and Jane go to concerts together.   59 B.
(b) Come and sit with Michael and (I, me).   59 B.
(c) The bull chased Ted and (I, me).   59 B.
(d) The cause (of, for) the damage (was, was due to) a
    sudden flood.   60
(e) He has no cause (of, for) complaint.   60
(f) I enclosed a (check, cheque) for ten pounds.   61
(g) Uncle gave me a choice between a holiday in Paris
    (and, or) a Mediterranean cruise.   62
(h) The bus does not (collect, gather, pick up) passengers
    at this corner.   69
(i) I shall (collect, call for) the suit this afternoon.   69

15. Select the correct item.   Section
(a) The audience (have, has) shown (its, their) approval.   70
(b) The committee (is, are) divided on the question of
    raising subscriptions.   70
(c) Truth is often compared (to, with) a beacon or a
    light.   75
(d) I usually compare one article (to, with) another to
    see which is the better value.   75
(e) Which of the two brothers is the (taller, tallest) ?   76
(f) Jane is the (more, most) attractive of the four
    sisters.   76
(g) The teacher asked the class to write a sentence
    containing a (compliment, complement).   77
(h) Sandra considered it a (compliment, complement) to
    be asked to dance with the guest of honour.   77
(i) The chief engineer is very concerned (with, about)
    the crack in the bridge girder.   79
(j) A geologist is concerned (with, about) the rocks of
    the Earth's crust.   79

16. Select the correct item.   Section
(a) Do you think it would be wise to confide (to, in)
    Harry?   81
(b) A (confidant, confident) player has an advantage
    over a nervous opponent.   82
(c) I was confronted (by, with) the necessity to find a
    job.   83

(d) I sent a telegram to congratulate Tom (on, for)
    passing his exams.   84
(e) Our team can win (providing, provided) that the
    wicket is dry.   85 C.
(f) John is much cleverer than (I, me).   85 C.
(g) They will be wondering (if, whether) we intend
    visiting them on Sunday.   85 C.
(h) Suddenly I decided to take up my pen and (contact,
    write to) him.   87
(i) Only a (contemptuous, contemptible) person would
    steal from a blind beggar.   88
(j) He spoke of his political rival in (contemptuous,
    contemptible) terms.   88

17. Write each sentence correctly.   Section
(a) The terrified man's face went as white like snow.   36
(b) I didn't have a clue about the last question, so I
    couldn't answer it.   67
(c) The jury has given its verdict; many people will
    disagree with their decision.   70
(d) On this subject old Mr Brown seems to have a bee
    in his bonnet.   71
(e) We had a fabulous time at the party; the band was
    tremendous.   73
(f) The camels having eaten the Arabs moved on.   74
(g) Their quarrel over the two men walked off in
    opposite directions.   74
(h) Which of these three rods is the stronger?   76
(i) Who is the cleverest of the Smith twins?   76
(j) The tool kit comprised of an electric drill, a saw,
    and a sanding disc.   78

18. (i) Compare the following sentences and paragraph with those
given as examples of incoherent writing in section **68 Coherence.**
(a) If he doesn't get his own way, he refuses to play with the other
    boys.
(b) After reading most of the plays, I have formed the opinion that
    King Lear is the most pathetic of Shakespeare's characters.
(c) The ranger, hoping to take a photo, stood in a stream with a few
    natives, trying to drive a lion out of the bushes in which it had
    taken shelter and into an open space.

(d) By midnight I was feeling cold and tired and so I decided to go to bed. Then I remembered that I had to finish some algebra. So, I made a cup of coffee, got a rug to keep me warm, and set to work.

(ii) Select the correct item.   Section
(a) We have hired two bands, so dancing will be (continual, continuous).   89
(b) (Continuous, Continual) interruptions have prevented me from finishing this report.   89
(c) Place the bulbs in a shallow trench and cover them (in, with, by) sandy soil.   91
(d) Such a strange story is hardly (creditable, credible).   92
(e) Winning an Olympic gold medal is a (creditable, credible) performance.   92

18. A. (i) Explain the difference in the meanings of each pair of sentences.   Section
(a) You also are invited to this party.   24
     You are invited to this party also.
(b) You have offended him, as well as I.   41
     You have offended him as well as me.
(ii) Select the correct item.
(a) I do not wish to play golf this morning; (beside, besides) I am too busy.   48
(b) The (burnt, burned) toast was thrown away.   55
(c) A great desire for power (burnt, burned) within him.   55
(d) (We, Us) girls love preparing meals.   59 B.
(e) It was (I, me) who spilt the ink.   59 B.
(f) I often see Ted and (he, him) on the bus.   59 B.
(g) He gave me the largest (half, portion) of the pie.   76
(h) This is the (more, most) flexible of the two rods.   76
(i) I had hardly sat down (than, when) the phone rang.   90

19. Write each sentence correctly.   Section
(a) Charles is heavier if not as tall as Jim.   85 C.
(b) I held the club like my tutor showed me.   85 C.
(c) The reason why John failed was because he spent too much time playing sport.   85 C.
(d) He says he likes neither ale or wine.   85 C.
(e) The children were tired, also they were very hungry.   85 C.
(f) Those young ruffians were not only insolent, but also they threatened us with violence.   90

(g) Rounding a sharp bend in the road a lovely view of the sea came into sight. 93
(h) Spouting water high into the air the excited passengers watched the whales. 93
(i) Equipped with all these fittings you will find this car most comfortable. 93
(j) To ride a bicycle your sense of balance must be good. 93

19. A. Write each sentence correctly. Section
(a) The reason why we are late is because our car broke down. 46
(b) Her physical attractions tended to be diminished by auditory appendages of abnormal magnitude. 64
(c) In supporting this candidate you appear to be flogging a dead horse. 71
(d) This rose is more perfect than that one. 76
(e) The surf is more rougher today than it was yesterday. 76
(f) A crocodile is as dangerous, if not more dangerous, than a shark. 85 C.
(g) The reason why I cannot come with you is because I have spent all my money. 85 C.
(h) No sooner had she entered the room when the cameras began to click. 85 C.
(i) Being well cooked on one side I turned the barbecue steak. 93
(j) Approaching the city a heavy fog and poor visibility reduced our speed. 93

20. Select the correct item. Section
(a) This event took place in the year (89 A.D.; A.D. 89). 96
(b) Queen Elizabeth's reign covered the period (from 1558 to 1603; from 1558–1603). 96
(c) All the (defective, deficient) articles were offered for sale at reduced prices. 97
(d) That shrub is dying because the soil is (defective, deficient) in potash. 97
(e) The accused produced evidence that (refuted, denied) the charge of corruption. 99
(f) Mr Brown is taxed lightly because he has six (dependents, dependants). 100

(g) I am still (dependent, dependant) upon my parents.   100
(h) My favourite (desert, dessert) is chocolate meringue.   101
(i) Your opinions on most social problems differ (to, from, than) mine.   102
(j) A person's political views may (differ, vary) according to his financial position.   102

21. Select the correct item.   Section
(a) The child said "I want to go home (now." now".)   103 B.
(b) The teacher said "Are you listening, (Tom?"; Tom"?)   103 B.
(c) Isaac Newton (invented, discovered) the nature of gravity.   104
(d) Marconi is given the credit for the (invention, discovery) of radio.   104
(e) I am disgusted (at, with) you.   105
(f) The health inspectors were disgusted (at, for) the condition of the streets.   105
(g) A referee should be interested in the progress of the game but (uninterested, disinterested) in the result.   106
(h) The aged gardener was afraid that he would be (replaced, displaced) by a stronger worker.   107
(i) A (distinct, distinctive) smell of gas was noticed in the bathroom.   109
(j) This brand of coffee has a (distinct, distinctive) flavour.   109

22. Select the correct item.   Section
(a) Has the (Dr, doctor) called yet?   110
(b) Has (Dr, Doctor) Green changed your medicine?   110
(c) The farmer said we wouldn't find (any, no) mushrooms in that field.   111
(d) I doubt (if, whether) our team can win today.   112
(e) The children have (drank, drunk) all the lemonade.   113
(f) The old man (drank, drunk) his tea in silence.   113
(g) Apparently the accident was (due, owing) to poor visibility.   114
(h) (Owing, Due) to the threatening weather, we left the beach early.   114
(i) Each man had (his, their) own task.   115
(j) Each of the boys (has, have) (his, their) own blankets.   115

23. Select the correct item. Section
(a) I found I could climb the rope quite (easy, easily). 117
(b) Mushrooms are (edible, eatable) but toadstools are
    not. 118
(c) These over-ripe bananas are not (edible, eatable). 118
(d) Thompson is a very (effective, efficient) foreman. 120
(e) This poison is very (effective, efficient) on flat weeds. 120
(f) Either of us (is, are) likely to be chosen. 121
(g) (Either, Any one) of these three books would
    interest you. 121
(h) Either Jane or Doris (is, are) willing to mind your
    baby. 122
(i) Neither Tom (or, nor) Harry (is, are) likely to win. 122
(j) An (eminent, imminent) sociologist spoke to us
    about the drug problem. 123
(k) As an election was (eminent, imminent) the politician
    returned to his electorate. 123

24. Select the correct item. Section
(a) We have had a month of (specially, especially)
    humid weather. 127
(b) Fred has written a humorous poem (specially,
    especially) for this occasion. 127
(c) Every student brought (his, their) microscope with
    (him, them). 130
(d) Everyone is expected to do (his, their) best to assist
    in this work. 131
(e) We won every match (except, excepting) the last. 132
(f) Jane said everybody was admitted except (she, her). 132
(g) The speed limit must be observed by everyone, not
    (except, excepting) the police. 132
(h) After an (exhaustive, exhausting) swim the lifesaver
    reached the upturned boat. 134
(i) An (exhaustive, exhausting) search for the missing
    will was in vain. 134
(j) He doesn't seem able to (face, face up to) even the
    smallest problem. 136

25. Write each sentence correctly. Section
(a) I cannot come to your party as I have a date on
    that evening. 95
(b) I am determined to definitely ask for a higher salary. 98

(c) The interviewer put the same question to three different people, and they all gave different answers. 102

(d) The drivers waited for each other to cross the intersection. 116

(e) The two cars followed each other slowly up the hill. 116

(f) When the cars met on the narrow track neither of the drivers would give way to each other. 116

(g) Enclosed herewith please find a cheque for fifty pounds. 124

(h) I can't tolerate that fellow's conceit. 125

(i) The foreman said he wouldn't endure my casual attitude any longer. 125

(j) Ann can run equally as fast as Jane. 126

25. A. Select the correct item. Section

(a) Newton is credited with the (invention, discovery) of the Law of Gravity. 104

(b) A judge should be (uninterested, disinterested) in the cases he has to try, but he should not be (uninterested, disinterested). 106

(c) At the beach we noticed a (distinct, distinctive) smell of oil, so we moved to a cleaner area. 109

(d) Has the baby (drank, drunk) her orange juice? 113

(e) The tropical north and the dry centre of the continent each (has, have) its own scenic attractions. 115

(f) My brother and I often borrow each (other's, others') car. 116

(g) Neither Fred nor Charles (is, are) (applicants, an applicant) for the job. 122

(h) The poet laureate composed an ode (specially, especially) for the occasion. 127

(i) Every musician prefers to use (their, his) own instrument. 130

(j) At last these unfortunate refugees are free (of, from) hunger. 144

26. Select the correct item. Section

(a) The guerillas were familiar (to, with) the mountains to which they retreated. 137

(b) It was then that he made the (fatal, serious) mistake which lost the game. 138

(c) The French Revolution was one of the (fatal, fateful) events of world history.   138

(d) Frank has had (less, fewer) opportunities than John.   140

(e) There were (less, fewer) members at the annual meeting this year.   140

(f) I wish my holiday could go on (for ever, forever).   142

(g) The refugees were glad to be at last free (of, from) persecution.   144

(h) We are pleased to send you these samples free (of, from) cost.   144

(i) The police took a gun (off, from) the prisoner.   145

(j) The baby drank two (cupsful, cupfuls) of milk.   146

(k) Take one (teaspoon full, teaspoonful) three times a day.   146

27. Select the correct item.   Section

(a) My mother does not approve of (me, my) staying out late.   148

(b) You have missed a (gold, golden) opportunity.   149

(c) She owns several valuable (gold, golden) bracelets.   149

(d) The swallow is very (graceful, gracious) in flight.   151

(e) The duchess was well known as a (graceful, gracious) hostess.   151

(f) Do you think criminals should be (hanged, hung?)   154

(g) I had hardly started to read (than, when) the light failed.   155

(h) A case of tomatoes (has, have) been left on the counter.   156

(i) The members, as well as the secretary, (has, have) to entertain the visitors.   156

(j) Is Tom in the picture? Yes, that is (he, him) in the middle of the back row.   157

27. A. Write each sentence correctly.   Section

(a) In what way is a crocodile different than an alligator?   102

(b) The manager told the clerk that he was sorry he had taken the money.   103 A.

(c) The farmer said he had never seen no red squirrels in that district.   111

(d) Due to a severe cold Mary missed her Science test.   114

(e) Either of them are capable of doing this job.   121

(f) My camera is equally as expensive as his.	126
(g) I appreciate his belated attempt to substantiate his statement rather than retaliate with more inaccurate accusations.	129
(h) Every one of these radios have a broken case.	131
(i) The teacher took the dangerous fireworks off the boys.	145
(j) I've got to go home now.	150

28. Select the correct item.   Section

(a) I have been told that colour-blindness is a (heredity, hereditary) condition.	158
(b) People who breed animals believe that (heredity, hereditary) is all-important.	158
(c) Ted's father disapproves of (him, his) smoking and drinking.	159
(d) Our (historic, historical) society is collecting pictures of Georgian houses.	161
(e) Many (historic, historical) documents can be seen in the museum.	161
(f) To improve your game you should (practice, practise) every day.	162
(g) Most of the (populace, populous) suffered in the epidemic.	162
(h) I believe this has been a (worth-while, worthwhile) effort.	163
(i) Take one (table-spoon-ful, tablespoonful) twice daily.	163
(j) Most people have their (downs and ups, ups and downs).	164
(k) We thought he would die (of, with) laughter.	164

29. Write each sentence correctly.   Section

(a) Mr Swigger is rather fond of the bottle; he is often seen under the weather.	128
(b) Stop that. You contemptible wretch.	133
(c) I have just heard a fabulous piece of gossip.	135
(d) Is it feasible that there will be a frost tonight?	139
(e) We are hoping to finalize arrangements by the end of this week.	141
(f) 'This talk should be interesting Do you know the speaker He is Mr J R Thomas B Sc	147

(g)	When I got a cold I got my mother to get some medicine from the chemist.	150
(h)	How many cousins have you got?	150
(i)	I guess he is sorry for what he has done.	152
(j)	It's a pity that vandalism has reared its ugly head in our town.	153

30. Select the correct item.   Section

(a)	I do not know (if, whether) the postman has called.	166
(b)	Please advise us immediately (if, whether) you wish us to reserve accommodation for you.	166
(c)	William Blake's poems and drawings are highly (imaginary, imaginative).	167
(d)	Stevenson wrote a story about an (imaginary, imaginative) place called Treasure Island.	167
(e)	The Chancellor's statement seems to (imply, infer) that taxes will be raised in the next budget.	168
(f)	From these comments I (imply, infer) that income tax will be increased.	168
(g)	Does this train stop (at, in) Derby?	169
(h)	We lived (at, in) London for two years.	169
(i)	John lives (at, in) 38 Spring Street; he previously lived (at, in) Main Road.	169
(j)	Lancashire was one of the first (industrious, industrial) regions.	170
(k)	John is a very (industrial, industrious) boy; he is never idle.	170

31. Select the correct item.   Section

(a)	Most paints and lacquers are (inflammatory, inflammable).	172
(b)	The judge (afflicted, inflicted) a severe punishment on the guilty man.	173
(c)	Poor Mrs Jones is (afflicted, inflicted) with lumbago.	173
(d)	In Asia rice is grown by (intense, intensive) cultivation.	176
(e)	(Ugh! Ah! Bravo!) That is bad news.	177
(f)	I found the working conditions (intolerant, intolerable) so I resigned.	179
(g)	Cheap trinkets of this kind are almost (invaluable, valueless).	180

151

(h) (Its, It's) such a cold day that our dog has not left
    (its, it's) kennel.   182
(i) Who is there? It is (I, me).   183

32. Write each sentence correctly.   Section
(a) Each entrant should bring their own bowls.   115
(b) This wool is of better than average quality.   163
(c) I shall travel abroad if and when I win the lottery.   165
(d) We are in receipt of your letter of 12th June.   174
(e) I thank you for your letter of 15th ult.   175
(f) In the event of your not being able to come, I shall
    take my young brother.   178
(g) Oliver said please sir I want some more   181
(h) He was accompanied by a member of the fair sex
    whose most conspicuous physical features were
    auditory appendages of great magnitude.   184 B.
(i) My friends say we should let sleeping dogs lie, but I
    am the man at the wheel and I shall leave no
    stone unturned to see that this man reaps the
    harvest he has sown.   184 C.
(j) He sort of sneered as we went past.   186

33. Select the correct item.   Section
(a) The Leader of the Opposition party asked for a
    (judicious, judicial) inquiry into the disappearance
    of the documents.   185
(b) His (judicious, judicial) remarks helped to prevent a
    serious quarrel.   185
(c) Do you like (this, these) sort of confectionery?   186
(d) All these (kind, kinds) of cigarettes make me cough.   186
(e) We were pleased to observe a complete (absence,
    lack) of selfishness in the children's actions.   187
(f) That log has (laid, lain) there for many years.   189
(g) This morning I (laid, lay) in the sun for two hours.   189
(h) The workmen (laid, lay) eight hundred bricks today.   189
(i) The drover told his dog to (lie, lay) down.   189
(j) Could you (learn, teach) a person to drive a car?   190

34. Select the correct item.   Section
(a) May I have a (lend, loan) of your mower?   191
(b) I never (lend, loan) money, and never borrow it.   191

(c) There are (less, fewer) opportunities for employment
in country areas.   192
(d) This year we sold a few more four-cylinder cars and
a few (less, fewer) six-cylinder models.   192
(e) Tom is (apt, liable) to make promises and then fail
to keep them.   193
(f) Jane is dark-skinned like you and (I, me).   195
(g) I have lost my watch. Please help me to (find,
locate) it.   196
(h) This nut is (loose, lose); if you don't tighten it, you
will (loose, lose) it.   197
(i) The visitors to Hawaii admired the (luxuriant,
luxurious) vegetation.   198
(j) He lives in a (luxuriant, luxurious) flat near the
harbour.   198

34. A. Select the correct item.   Section
(a) The injured man was able to swallow several
(mouthsfull, mouthfuls) of water.   146
(b) My parents disliked (me, my) leaving home.   148
(c) Many people believe that baldness is (heredity,
hereditary).   158
(d) Jane worked (at, in) a snack bar, but now she is a typist
(at, in) the Public Library.   169
(e) The rebel leader's (inflammable, inflammatory)
remarks soon had the crowd shouting for revenge.   172
(f) The opposite of 'invaluable' is ('valuable',
'valueless').   180
(g) Mary asked me to bring her racquet; is this (hers,
her's)?   182
(h) I (lay, laid) on the lawn till the bell rang.   189
(i) "That will (learn, teach) you!" said the policeman.   190
(j) My deaf aunt is always (liable, apt) to imagine that
people are talking about her.   193

35. Select the correct item.   Section
(a) Bad manners (is, are) a common fault in young
people.   199
(b) Mathematics (have, has) always been my weakest
subject.   199
(c) I thought I (may, might) have to wait, so I took a
book to read.   200

(d) (Maybe, Perhaps) I shall see you here at the show
next year. 201
(e) It was (I, me) who was to blame. 202
(f) The defenders of castles poured (melted, molten)
lead upon the attacking forces. 203
(g) I'm afraid the chocolates have (melted, molten) in
the sun. 203
(h) Although we enjoyed our picnic, (somebody's transistor
radio, a wasps' nest) was a great menace. 204
(i) I move that Miss Brown (is, be) appointed Secretary. 206
(j) Jane's dress was (much, very) admired at the ball. 208
(k) He gives two explanations, but neither (are, is)
satisfactory. 210

36. Write each sentence correctly. Section
(a) Russia, China and Japan have recently increased
their trade with Australia, especially the latter. 188
(b) The car in which the child was sleeping was guarded
by a large dog. The latter snarled whenever
anyone approached. 188
(c) Hold the club like your coach suggested. 195
(d) There is no need to put our heads in the sand and
throw up the sponge. 205
(e) Mrs Wright and Smith have been elected to the
committee. 207
(f) I believe myself that young people have too much
freedom. 209
(g) John and Peter are expected at the party, but neither
of them have yet arrived. 210
(h) Tom said I broke the window but I never did. 212
(i) I never went to the barbecue last week-end. 212
(j) We saw a very nice film last night. 213

36. A. Write each sentence correctly. Section
(a) The teacher, as well as the pupils are travelling on
the bus. 156
(b) Each student must return his or her report book to
the office. 160
(c) Tom laughed allowed, and the teacher looked
angrily at him. 162
(d) I am afraid our efforts have not been worth-while. 163
(e) Your remarks seem to infer that he is concealing
the truth. 168

(f) Do you like these sort of apples?	186
(g) Grandma laid down to rest for a while.	189
(h) What this business needs is a few more customers and a few fewer employees.	192
(i) It looks like they are not coming.	195
(j) Inflation is again rearing its ugly head, and unless we nip it in the bud it will lead to an explosion that will deluge the whole country.	205

37. Select the correct item.   Section

(a) (None, Neither) of the three brothers has
    distinguished himself.   210

(b) Neither John nor Frank (have, has) offered to help.   210

(c) Nobody likes to be wrongly accused, (does he, do
    they)?   214

(d) Nobody wishes to hear what gossips are saying
    about (him, them).   214

(e) None of the accusations (was, were) supported by
    evidence.   215

(f) None of those sheep (has, have) been shorn yet.   215

(g) We had no sooner set off (when, than) a front tyre
    went flat.   216

(h) It was a (notable, notorious) speech, deserving of
    the applause that followed.   217

(i) The number of emigrants going to Australia (have, has)
    risen in recent years.   221

(j) A number of sheep (was, were) seen grazing in the
    fields.   221

38. Write each sentence correctly.   Section

(a) The police not only searched the house thoroughly
    but also the nearby park.   218

(b) I seem to have lost my key. Oh well, not to worry.   219

(c) The two hundred and 50 mile race will finish at
    about 20 minutes past four. Five or 6 cars are on
    their last lap.   222

(d) He only gave his autograph to one of the hundreds
    of boys surrounding him.   226

(e) The diamond is harder than any gemstone.   227

(f) After a trial period of three months we shall consider
    the success or otherwise of our venture.   229

(g) Looking up, the shower had stopped, so we set off.   230

(h) Being a holiday, we decided to go fishing.   230
(i)   The cost is six pounds per square yard, delivered to your
      home per parcel post.   233
(j)   I should have liked to have seen the Niagara Falls.   234
(k) If I had have known you were waiting, I would have
      hurried.   234

39. Select the correct item.   Section
(a) The (occupant, occupier) of the front seat handed
      her fare to the conductress.   223
(b) A public servant should perform his (official,
      officious) duties carefully but not (officially,
      officiously).   224
(c) One should always be loyal to (his, one's) friends.   225
(d) I did not punish the child; (on the contrary, on the
      other hand) I praised him for his honesty in
      admitting his fault.   228
(e) This car is cheaper to buy than that one; (on the
      contrary, on the other hand) it is more expensive
      to maintain.   228
(f) You will have to work harder, or (else, otherwise)
      you will fail.   229
(g) I (past, passed) the butter to my brother.   232
(h) The children hurried (past, passed) the haunted
      house.   232
(i)   All his (personal, personnel) belongings were lost in
      the fire.   236
(j)   All (personal, personnel) employed by this company
      must contribute to the welfare fund.   236

40. Write each sentence correctly.   Section
(a) Personally I do not care for sweet wines.   235
(b) My personal opinion is that our team will win easily.   235
(c) Spouting water into the air the tourists saw a
      number of whales on their way to visit the art
      galleries of Europe.   237 B.
(d) The formulas were incorrect as I had been given data
      which was confused.   238
(e) The inquiry was conducted by four Justice of the
      Peaces.   238
(f) Take advantage of our reduced prices plus generous
      trade-in allowances.   239

(g) The officer said that mine and your cars were
    illegally parked.   241
(h) It seems that his and my viewpoints are similar.   241
(i) Do you think it is more preferable to tell a lie
    rather than to betray a friend?   245
(j) This adds rather than detracts from the strength of
    your argument.   246 B.
(k) The compartment in which we travelled in was not
    very comfortable.   246 B.

41. Select the correct item.   Section
(a) The new teachers are both (M.A.s, Ms.A.).   238
(b) Thieves have stolen Mr (Baker's, Bakers') car.   240
(c) That is my (brother's-in-laws, brother-in-law's)
    home.   240
(d) There was a happy look on the (boy's, boys') faces. 240
(e) Have you put away the (childrens', children's) toys? 240
(f) The dog is sleeping in (its, it's) kennel.   240
(g) Applicants should have a (practical, practicable)
    knowledge of the trade.   242
(h) Your idea for the summer fête is original but not
    (practical, practicable).   242
(i) I (practice, practise) for two hours each day.   243
(j) You need more (practice, practise) to improve your
    game.   243

42. Select the correct item.   Section
(a) In formal processions the Queen (proceeds, precedes)
    all other persons.   244
(b) Most children prefer lemonade (than, to) tea or
    coffee.   245
(c) I must congratulate Tom (for, on) passing his
    examinations.   246
(d) Plans for a house must comply (to, with) the
    building regulations.   246
(e) This soil is deficient (in, of) potash.   246
(f) These plants are very sensitive (to, with) the cold. 246
(g) The boys threw stones at John and (I, me).   246 B.
(h) Sit here between Jane and (I, me).   246 B.
(i) Shakespeare compared a woman's beauty (to, with)
    a summer's day.   246

(j) These two machines work on the same (principal, principle).   247

(k) His (principal, principle) aim in life is to become rich.   247

43. Select the correct item.   Section

(a) Tom says I am not as tall as (he, him).   249 C.

(b) Every man is expected to do (their, his) share.   249 D.

(c) Each attended to (his, their) own allotted task.   249 D.

(d) Either John or Henry (is, are) waving to us.   249 D.

(e) Neither of these applicants (is, are) qualified for the job.   249 D.

(f) John passed his exams because he worked (purposely, purposefully) and systematically.   252

(g) He said, "Why do you look so (surprised"?, surprised?")   255

(h) Facts about social problems are often gathered by means of a (quiz, questionnaire).   257

(i) The sun has already (rose, risen).   259

(j) Have they (raised, risen) the sunken boat?   259

(k) An awkward situation (rose, arose) when the two rivals came face to face.   259

44. Write each sentence correctly.   Section

(a) I shall visit a friend in hospital prior to going to the party.   248

(b) When the boy caught up with the burglar, he hit him.   249 B.

(c) After the baby has finished its bottle wash it thoroughly.   249 B.

(d) Clear the staff from the offices and fumigate them.   249 B.

(e) Friends offered to take Mother and myself to the barbecue.   249 C.

(f) The Mirage is a French military plane; they are also built in Australia.   249 C.

(g) I, you and she are selected in the same team.   249 D.

(h) Many rumours have been spread about the staff which are quite ridiculous.   250

(i) Farmer Brown found a nest of fieldmice harvesting his crop.   250

(j) A number of dolphins were seen by the excited passengers leaping out of the water.   250

45. Write each sentence correctly.   Section

(a) I queried the postal clerk about closing times for
    outward mail.   253

(b) You mentioned qualifications. We shall discuss that
    question later.   254

(c) Thank you for helping with our programme. I thought
    your playing was quite good.   256

(d) "Will you please turn down the volume, Anne" asked
    John?   258

(e) He said My name is Bill but I am called Ocker by
    my mates.   258

(f) That hole in the footpath is a real danger to
    pedestrians.   261

(g) Our guest artist gave a really fine performance.   261

(h) I see no cause for undue pessimism at this point of
    time.   264

(i) I want to take this opportunity to thank you for
    your generosity in giving so freely of your time
    and services.   264

(j) When the watchman surprised the thief he aimed a
    pistol at his heart which he had concealed in his
    coat pocket.   267

(k) The boys caught several rabbits which pleased the
    gardener.   267

46. Select the correct item.   Section

(a) I wish to inquire (re, about) the advertised vacancy
    on your staff.   260

(b) We intend to have our old arm-chair (recovered,
    re-covered).   263

(c) You should not feel (regretful, regrettable) over
    such a small accident, especially as the outcome
    was humorous rather than (regretful, regrettable).   266

(d) Modern printing techniques make possible the
    production of near-perfect (replicas, copies) of
    the works of old masters.   268

(e) The (Reverent, Reverend) Charles Forsyth will
    conduct the evening service.   270

(f) I have to write a (review, revue) of this novel. I
    would prefer to be going with you to the
    music-hall (review, revue).   271

(g) The plane had scarcely left the ground (when, than) there was a loud explosion. 273

(h) As for the existence of ghosts, I must say I am a (sceptic, septic) on that subject. 274

(i) Autumn clothed the poplars in garments of red and gold (, ;) winter hung them with crystal beads of ice. 275

(j) The only movement was the (quivering, shudder, vibration) of the reeds in the breeze. 278

(k) He intends to (revive, reinstate, renovate) the old oak chest. 278

46. A. Write each sentence correctly. Section

(a) The people next door have a nice dog. 213

(b) 90% of the forty students in Form V passed in 4 or more subjects. 222

(c) My grandmother only died last week. 226

(d) Having read several good reference books, my essay will now be easy to write. 230

(e) Coming home, an accident blocked the road and delayed us. 230

(f) The commander-in-chiefs met to plan their strategy. 238

(g) Thanks to yours and my efforts we have succeeded. 241

(h) Why did you say, "You will live to regret this?" 255

(i) The result of his foolishness was that it led to his death. 264

(j) Can you tell me who was the first originator of the telephone? 264

47. Select the correct item. Section

(a) I am determined that he (shall, will) apologize for his rudeness. 279

(b) I (shall, will) go with you if you wish me to. 279

(c) Statistics (is, are) an interesting branch of mathematics. 282

(d) What caused the accident (was, were) two trees that had fallen across the road. 282

(e) A number of children (was, were) waiting for their teacher. 282

(f) The number of members present (is, are) very disappointing. 282

(g) Three months (is, are) a long time to spend in hospital. 282

(h) One of the watches (was, were) damaged. 282

(i) He is one of those boys who (is, are) always trying
   to attract attention. 282

(j) Fred finished his homework early so (as, that) he
   could watch the television serial. 284

48. Select the correct item. Section

(a) The poorer people wore (course, coarse) (woolen, woollen)
   garments. 286

(b) The letter ended with the words, 'Yours (truly,
   truely)'. 286

(c) We still have (fourty, forty) miles to go. 286

(d) I am sorry the shower (spoilt, spoiled) your picnic. 288

(e) I am afraid Charles is a (spoilt, spoiled) child. 288

(f) The car crashed into the rear end of a (stationery,
   stationary) bus. 289

(g) In cases of minor illness brandy is often used as a
   (stimulus, stimulant). 290

(h) The offer of higher wages was an effective (stimulus,
   stimulant) to the fruit-pickers. 290

(i) I hope the bus (stays, stops) for a while at Doncaster. 291

(j) The injured man is still (unconscious, subconscious). 294

(k) Psychiatrists try to help emotionally disturbed people
   by exploring the (unconscious, subconscious)
   mind. 294

(l) In examinations, it is better to use (new and
   unconventional language, established and
   conventional language). 292

49. Write each sentence correctly. Section

(a) Please complete the enclosed form and return same
   within seven days. 272

(b) He was hardly out of sight than I remembered who
   he was. 273

(c) A buffalo charged at the hunter and he took refuge
   in a tree. 277 C.

(d) We should be pleased if you will call and discuss
   the matter. 280

(e) The night was as black as ink and as cold as ice. 281

(f) He dashed off a quick note to the chap he'd been with at the
   local before the row broke out. 283

161

(g) He promised to always under all circumstances
     consider my best interests.   287
(h) I am going to stop with friends in Brighton.   291
(i) Some of the children were amused by the monkeys
     such as Tommy and Ted.   296
(j) The lorry carried bricks, tiles, drainage pipes and
     such like.   296
(k) We have been informed that you do not intend to return.
     Please advise us whether such is the case.   296

50. Select the correct item.   Section
(a) We are experiencing serious economic depression,
     (subsequent to, consequent on) a number of
     widespread strikes.   295
(b) While on holiday Mr Moneybags was (summonsed,
     summoned) to a meeting of shareholders.   297
(c) Yesterday I received a (summon, summons) for a
     traffic offence.   297
(d) We tried to (abolish, exterminate, extinguish,
     demolish, obliterate) the ants which were getting
     into the pantry.   298
(e) I (rang, rung) the doorbell several times.   300
(f) Has Frank (did, done) his homework?   300
(g) Jane has (sang, sung) that song many times.   300
(h) The river has (overflown, overflowed) its banks.   300
(i) Ted is two inches taller than (I, me).   301
(j) You can do this better than (he, him).   301

51. Write each sentence correctly.   Section
(a) The ancient castle we visited is very old.   299
(b) The Principal decided to combine the two small
     classes into one.   299
(c) Your sketch is equally as good as mine.   299
(d) Just then the umpire blows his whistle and awarded a
     free kick to my opponent.   300 B.
(e) We found more mushrooms than what we expected.   301
(f) The climb up Ayers Rock was that steep we were
     exhausted.   302
(g) The Queen and Duchess of Kent enjoyed the races.   303
(h) Both the employers and workers were dis-satisfied with
     the court's decision.   303
(i) Did you think to post my letters?   306
(j) Many market gardens were ruined, thus causing a

rise in the price of vegetables.   307

51. A. Select the correct item.   Section
(a) I (may, might) have to wait, so I'll take a book to
    read.   200
(b) Holidays are (past, passed); now we return to work.   232
(c) We ran to help the man (who, whom), it was plain
    to see, was badly injured.   267
(d) If you were not so (sceptical, cynical), you would
    realize that he acted from unselfish motives.   274
(e) After the lights failed we had to (abbreviate, abridge,
    curtail) the concert programme.   278
(f) Have you ever (swam, swum) a mile?   300
(g) The birds have (flew, flown) into the basement?   300
(h) Has the water (flowed, flown) into the basement?   300
(i) The baby has (drunk, drank) most of the milk.   300

52. Select the correct item.   Section
(a) The pups have eaten (they're, their, there) meat.   304
(b) Our visitors are early; (there, their, they're) at the
    door now.   304
(c) There (is, are) only two hours to wait.   305
(d) There are (too, two) men waiting (to, too) see you;
    a lady is waiting (two, too, to).   309
(e) I shall try (and, to) get a ticket for the concert.   310
(f) After eating all the meat the starving dog was still
    (dissatisfied, unsatisfied).   316
(g) You are treated generously; why are you so
    (dissatisfied, unsatisfied)?   316
(h) A fandango is a (tropical fruit, dance, weapon).   317
(i) The *hoi polloi* were the (wealthy, common) people
    of Greece.   317
(j) 'Comparable' is pronounced with the accent on the
    (first, second) syllable.   317

52. A. Write each sentence correctly.   Section
(a) The applicants were interviewed by the secretary,
    the manager, and the accountant respectively.   269
(b) The delegates gave their respective viewpoints.   269
(c) Beethoven, Mozart and Verdi lived in Germany and
    Italy respectively.   269
(d) Knowing that it was dangerous to remain on the
    rock ledge, and deciding to climb higher up to
    safety, which we did without much trouble.   276

163

(e) There were many incidents which looking back they
must have been very humorous at the time. 276
(f) Owing to bad weather during the last week of the
vacation and so we had little swimming. 276
(g) The explorers tried in vain to scale the cliffs, but
they were unable to do so. 299
(h) We were discouraged, but one fact however saved
us from despair. 299
(i) Rare species such as this are seldom seen. 299
(j) Fred Smith, the union secretary, spoke to the striking
workmen and has left for a holiday in Blackpool. 314

53. Write each sentence correctly. Section
(a) Did you like Da Vinci's Last Supper? 308
(b) It isn't unduly late, so we'll have another game. 311
(c) There is no cause for undue pessimism at present. 311
(d) Come early for our many unique bargains. 313
(e) This rose is fairly perfect, but that one is very
perfect. 313
(f) Today I met Frank Johnson who didn't look very
well and has just started work in a new position. 314
(g) I have booked to fly to San Francisco via Pan-
American Airways. 320
(h) What are they hurrying for? 326
(i) The rain forced us to postpone the picnic which
disappointed the children. 329
(j) The rhinoceros is an animal with a single large horn
and which has a very tough skin. 330

54. Select the correct item. Section
(a) Ann has (did, done) her homework. 318 B.
(b) Have you ever (swam, swum) the full length of the
pool? 318 B.
(c) The concert has just (begun, began). 318 B.
(d) The cat has not (drank, drunk) its milk. 318 B.
(e) I (rung, rang) my friend to tell him the good news. 318 B.
(f) That subject is (much, very) discussed among
students. 319
(g) I was (much, very) disappointed at the result of our
membership campaign. 319

(h) Food and clothing have been sent to the earthquake area with a view to (relieve, relieving) the distress there. 321

(i) In the sentence, 'The thief **was punished** for his crime', the verb is in the (active, passive) voice. 322

55. Write each sentence correctly. Section

(a) To who are you writing? 331 A.

(b) Whom did he say he is? 331 A.

(c) We ran to help the man whom, we feared, was badly injured. 331 B.

(d) I went to the city with a view to consult my legal adviser. 334

(e) The skater almost flew along, without hardly touching the ice. 335

(f) With reference to your letter of 5th May in reference to repairs to your tractor, we shall be pleased to do this work. 336

(g) I often wonder why you are so impatient? 337

(h) I am sure he would of helped if you had asked him to. 338

(i) When I asked him how far it was to the next town he replied, "I wouldn't know". 339

(j) They blame you and I. 340

(k) Fred says that you and me are selected in the team. . 340

56. Select the correct item. Section

(a) Ten members worked (voluntary, voluntarily) to prepare the courts for the tennis tournament. 323

(b) The prisoner anxiously (waited, awaited) the jury's verdict. 324

(c) Arriving home late, we found an urgent telegram (waiting, awaiting) us. 324

(d) Great honour (waits, awaits) the man who solves this problem. 324

(e) In arid areas the (wasting, wastage) of water is discouraged. 325

(f) In summer, evaporation causes a serious (waste, wastage) of water. 325

(g) The police say the suspect's whereabouts (is, are) not known. 327

(h) (What, Which) bird is that? 330

(i) (What, Which) of the two cars did he buy? 330

165

57. Select the correct item.   Section

(a) To (who, whom) did you give the message?   331 A.

(b) Do you know (who, whom) he is?   331 A.

(c) Please see (who's, whose) ringing the bell.   332

(d) Do you know (who's, whose) car this is?   332

(e) I would (of, have) hurried if I had known you were
   waiting.   338

(f) You and (I, me) are to sit at the same table.   340

(g) These books have been sent to you and (I, me) by
   the publisher.   340

(h) Will you please lend me (you're, your) pen?   341

(i) This is my lunch; that is (your's, yours).   341

COMMON ERRORS

The sentences included in Exercises **A.** to **L.** below cover points of usage on which errors are frequently made.

Each sentence should be completed correctly by the selection of the appropriate item from the alternatives given within brackets.

An answer section (page 172-3) gives the correct item for each sentence, and a number indicates the entry in the Dictionary that explains the point of usage involved.

These exercises and answers enable a student to test his ability to use correct English and so **determine the use he should make of the Study Guide [page 4] and the Dictionary.**

A. Nouns
(a) The constable asked for my driver's (license, licence).
(b) I haven't (a clue, any idea) how I can pay this debt.
(c) This recipe requires one (spoonful, spoon full) of cinnamon.
(d) Was the rabbit in the magician's hat, or was it an (allusion, illusion, delusion)?
(e) A reduction in VAT would be a strong (stimulus, stimulant) to business.
(f) (That sort, Those sort) of tree is too large for my garden.
(g) Mr Jones bought expensive presents for his two (daughter-in-laws, daughters-in-law).
(h) We hope to visit France next (autumn, Autumn).
(i) The final match of the (womens', women's) tennis will be played on the centre court.
(j) A man's *alma mater* is his (occupation, school, grandmother).

B. Pronouns
(a) (Anyone, Any one) of you could become lost in that forest.
(b) Has anyone a dictionary (he, they) can lend me?
(c) Freda and (I, me) live in the same street.
(d) Are you coming with Ted and (I, me)?
(e) (She and I, Her and me) often go surfing together.
(f) A lost dog followed (she and I, her and me).
(g) You are not as tall as (I, me).

(h) The high cost of living affects you as well as (I, me).
(i) Neither of the hunters saw (each other, the other).
(j) Did the manager approve of (your, you) being dismissed?

C. Pronouns
(a) Who broke this mirror? It was (I, me).
(b) My sister and (myself, I) usually like the same books.
(c) Two girls have applied, but neither (is, are) well qualified.
(d) (You, I and he; He, you and I) have been elected to the committee.
(e) (Who, Whom) did you accompany to the graduation ceremony?
(f) (Who, Whom) do you think he is?
(g) The boy (who, whom) we thought was lost was sitting in the bus.
(h) Our hostess (who, whom) we thought we had offended, came into the room smiling.
(i) (Who's, Whose) pen is this?
(j) (Who's, Whose) coming for a swim this morning?
(k) I believe this knife is (yours, your's).

D. Verbs
(a) You need to (practise, practice) at least an hour each day.
(b) Many plants are (affected, effected) by a shortage of water.
(c) A Canadian is credited with having (invented, discovered) the telephone.
(d) The lost explorers had to (endure, tolerate) many hardships.
(e) The Treasurer's remarks (inferred, implied) that the club's money had been wasted.
(f) After searching for an hour the mechanic (found, located) the missing valve.
(g) My shoe lace has become (lose, loose).
(h) Mother decided to (recover, re-cover) the comfortable but shabby armchair.
(i) Because we arrived late we (missed, missed out on) our supper.
(j) (Its, It's) a pity that rain spoilt the picnic.
(k) Did your flat-mate (approve, approve of) your choice of carpet?
(l) The coach, as well as the players, (was, were) surprised by the easy victory.

E. Verbs
(a) Dad, (may, can) I borrow your pocket calculator tomorrow?
(b) I asked if I (may, might) borrow his torch.
(c) Have the guests (drank, drunk) all the wine?

(d) I bought some poison to (annihilate, exterminate, obliterate) the troublesome ants.
(e) The drover shouted, "(Lay, Lie) down, Lassie."
(f) The children (lay, laid) on the grass till the picnic lunch was ready.
(g) That rusted anchor has (laid, lain) there near the cliff for many years.
(h) I should (like, have liked) to have visited Norway.
(i) My father would have been pleased (to meet, to have met) you.
(j) The moon had (rose, risen) before we arrived.
(k) I think you should (of, have) called for help earlier.
(l) I am glad (you're, your) coming fishing with us.

F. Agreement
(a) Egg and bacon (is, are) a popular breakfast dish.
(b) (Have, Has) my aunt and uncle arrived yet?
(c) 'Two Gentlemen of Verona' (are, is) my favourite play.
(d) A pack of cards (was, were) lying on the table.
(e) The jury has returned to give (its, their) verdict.
(f) Each member of the team (was, were) given a trophy.
(g) Either of the applicants (is, are) suitable for the position.
(h) Every one of these cameras (are, is) damaged.
(i) A number of parents (has, have) gathered outside the school.
(j) Twenty pounds (was, were) a heavy fine for such a trivial offence.
(k) He is one of those young fellows who (is, are) always looking for an argument.
(l) There (is, are) ten pounds to pay on delivery.

G. Adjectives
(a) Mother gave the biggest (half, piece) of the pie to the beggar.
(b) Iron is (much, more) heavier than aluminium.
(c) I thought the (two first, first two) chapters were the most interesting.
(d) Take (them, those) boxes to the delivery van.
(e) I had a (chronic, severe) toothache this morning.
(f) He became bankrupt because of a (fatal, serious) error of judgment.
(g) The critics say she is not an (imaginative, imaginary) writer.
(h) I work and have the day free on (alternate, alternative) Saturdays.
(i) We are all (confidant, confident) of success.
(j) Our picnic was spoilt by (terrible, wet and windy) weather.

(k) The (principal, principle) performers were entertained by the mayor.
(l) A motorist should take care when passing a (stationary, stationery) bus.

H. Adjectives
(a) The referee should be (disinterested, uninterested) in the result of a boxing bout.
(b) We received a Christmas card from the (Reverent, Reverend) John Gray.
(c) The canary is sitting on (its, it's) nest.
(d) Bring me the (longer, longest) of the two rods.
(e) The police found a (distinctive, distinct) smell of marihuana in the room.
(f) The over-cooked barbecue steak was not (eatable, edible).
(g) A mild manner is often more (judicial, judicious) than aggression.
(h) Each child has (his, their) own towel.
(i) The police asked every witness to give (their, his) opinion.
(j) There were (fewer, less) applicants than we expected.
(k) This bloom is (nearer to perfection, more perfect) than that one.

J. Adverbs
(a) The dentist spoke very (quiet, quietly) to the nervous child.
(b) Jane took care to write her application as (neat, neatly) as possible.
(c) We (didn't catch, never caught) (no, any) fish last week-end.
(d) After forty years of service my father (only retired, retired only) last week.
(e) The injured man was (so, that) weak that we had to support him.
(f) When we arrived the meeting had (all ready, already) started.
(g) We are (awfully, very) pleased to hear that you are well again.
(h) (It looks like, Apparently) we have missed the first event.
(i) The lost explorers hadn't had (anything, nothing) to eat for three days.
(j) This cake was made (specially, especially) for our anniversary.
(k) We waited till the funeral had gone (passed, past).
(l) Mrs Green's roses are always (much, very) admired.

K. Conjunctions
(a) The reason for your failure is (because, that) you were over-confident.
(b) The winner was asked to choose between a clock (and, or) a radio.

(c) You are not holding the club (like, as) the coach showed you.

(d) (It appears that, It looks like) we have taken the wrong road.

(e) I'll lend you my racquet (providing, provided that) you return it before Saturday.

(f) Some insects can neither hear (or, nor) see.

(g) Neither Jones (or, nor) Smith (has, have) been elected.

(h) We had hardly turned the first corner (than, when) a front tyre went flat.

(i) I had no sooner closed the door (than, when) a loud explosion shook the house.

(j) The yacht had scarcely left the pier (when, than) it was overturned by a gust of wind.

L. Prepositions

(a) Two shrubs were planted (between each tree, between trees).

(b) This plane carries three passengers (besides, beside) the pilot.

(c) The painting set (comprised, comprised of) colours, brushes, and canvases of different sizes.

(d) I often confide (in, to) my older brother.

(e) I sent a telegram to congratulate Michael (on, for) winning a scholarship.

(f) Is an alligator different (from, than) a crocodile?

(g) All people should be free (of, from) fear and hunger.

(h) Such behaviour is alien (to, from) his nature.

(i) Is that the ship to which your sailor friend (referred, referred to)?

(j) There were several collisions (due to, owing to) slippery roads.

171

Answers to Exercises **A.** *to* **L.**

Exercise A.
(a) licence **14**   (b) any idea **67**   (c) spoonful **146**   (d) illusion **162**
(e) stimulus **290**   (f) that sort **186**   (g) daughters-in-law **238**
(h) autumn **58**   (i) women's **240**   (j) school **317**

Exercise B.
(a) Any one **33**   (b) he **33**   (c) I **59**   (d) me **59**   (e) She and I **59**
(f) her and me **59**   (g) I **85**   (h) me **41**   (i) the other **116**
(j) your **148**

Exercise C.
(a) I **183**   (b) I **249**   (c) is **249**   (d) He, you and I **249**
(e) Whom **331**   (f) Who **331**   (g) who **331**   (h) whom **331**
(i) Whose **332**   (j) Who's **332**   (k) yours **341**

Exercise D.
(a) practise **14**   (b) affected **15**   (c) invented **104**   (d) endure **125**
(e) implied **168**   (f) found **196**   (g) loose **197**   (h) re-cover **263**
(i) missed **136**   (j) It's **34**   (k) approve of **35**   (l) was **41**

Exercise E.
(a) may **57**   (b) might **57**   (c) drunk **113**   (d) exterminate **278**
(e) Lie **189**   (f) lay **189**   (g) lain **189**   (h) like **234**   (i) to meet **234**
(j) risen **259**   (k) have **338**   (l) you're **341**

Exercise F.
(a) is **18**   (b) Have **18**   (c) is **18**   (d) was **18**   (e) its **70**
(f) was **111**   (g) is **121**   (h) is **131**   (i) have **221**   (j) was **282**
(k) are **282**   (l) is **305**

Exercise G.
(a) piece **10**   (b) much **10**   (c) first two **10**   (d) those **10**
(e) severe **63**   (f) serious **138**   (g) imaginative **167**
(h) alternate **25**   (i) confident **81**   (j) wet and windy **42**
(k) principal **247**   (l) stationary **289**

Exercise H.
(a) disinterested **106**   (b) Reverend **270**   (c) its **34**   (d) longer **76**
(e) distinct **109**   (f) eatable **118**   (g) judicious **185**   (h) his **115**
(i) his **130**   (j) fewer **140**   (k) nearer to perfection **76**

Exercise J.
(a) quietly **12**   (b) neatly **13**   (c) didn't catch any **12**
(d) retired only **12**   (e) so **12**   (f) already **20**   (g) very **42**
(h) Apparently **85**   (i) anything **111**   (j) specially **127**
(k) past **232**   (l) much **319**

Exercise K.
(a) that **46**   (b) and **50**   (c) as **85**   (d) It appears that **85**
(e) provided that **85**   (f) nor **90**   (g) nor . . . has **122**
(h) when **155**   (i) than **216**   (j) when **273**

Exercise L.
(a) between trees **27**   (b) besides **48**   (c) comprised **78**   (d) in **81**
(e) on **84**   (f) from **102**   (g) from **144**   (h) to **246**   (i) referred **246**
(j) owing to **114**